FRANCIS FRITH'S

WELLINGBOROUGH

LIVING MEMORIES

Martin Andrew is an architectural and landscape historian and writer on outdoor matters who is the Conservation Officer for Wycombe District Council in Buckinghamshire. He specialises in the landscape of Midland England and combines his love of history, landscape and architecture in his writing. Since 1978 he has lived in Haddenham in Buckinghamshire with his wife and children. He is a keen long distance walker and enjoys riding his classic motor cycle round the country lanes of Buckinghamshire, Oxfordshire and Northamptonshire. He was born in Doncaster, and he knows Northamptonshire well; besides walking many of its footpaths and bridleways he has written on its history. After university he worked for the Greater London Council's Historic Buildings Division, Buckinghamshire County Council, and Salisbury District Council before joining Wycombe District Council in 1990.

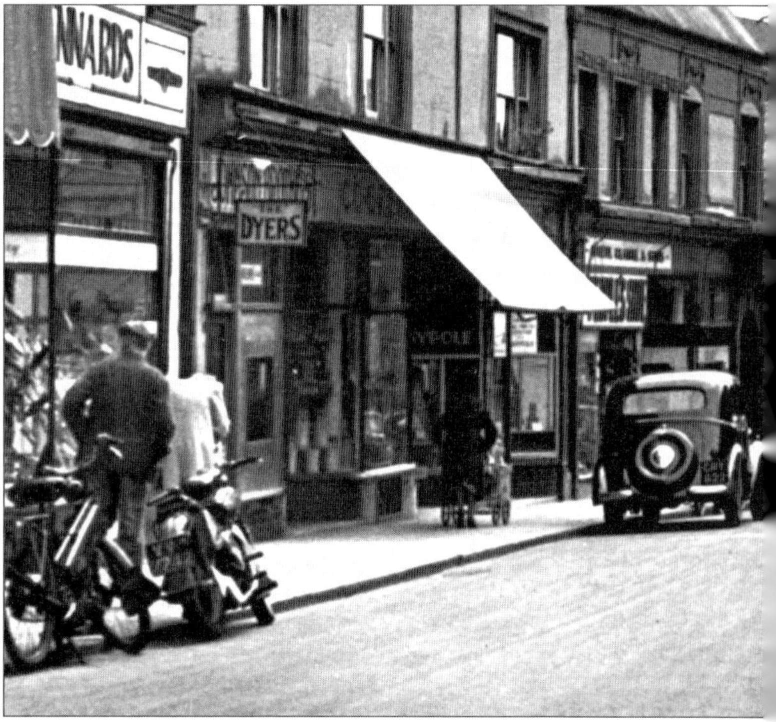

FRANCIS FRITH'S

PHOTOGRAPHIC MEMORIES

WELLINGBOROUGH
LIVING MEMORIES

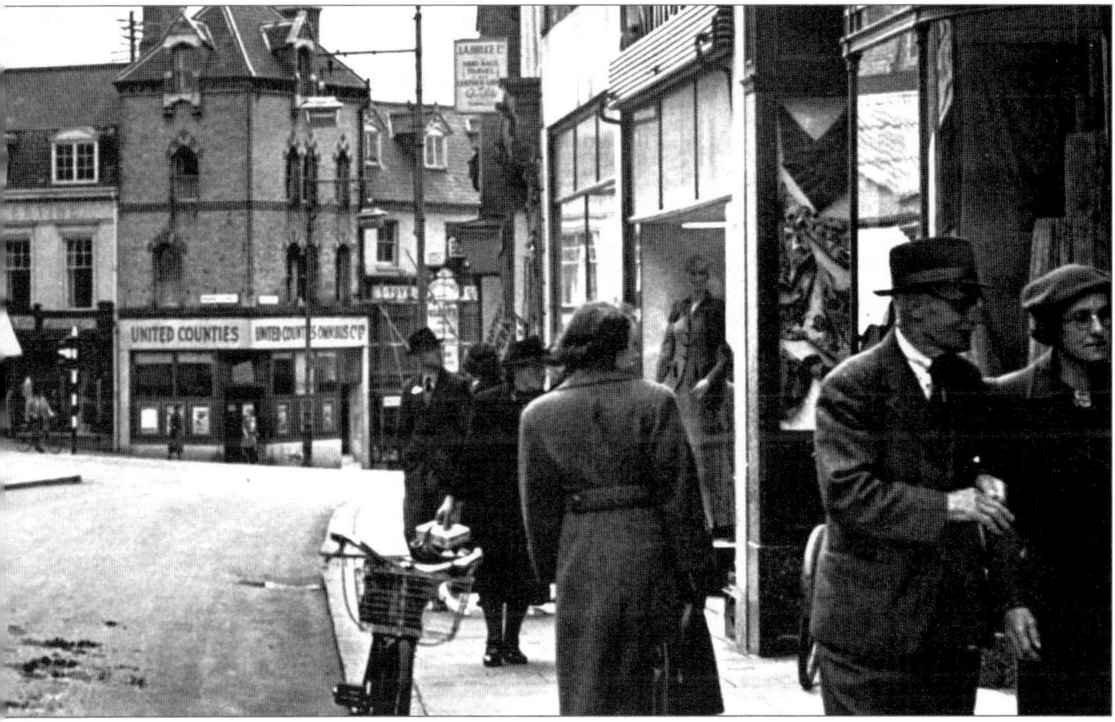

MARTIN ANDREW

First published in the United Kingdom in 2004 by
Frith Book Company Ltd

Hardback Limited Subscribers Edition 2004
ISBN 1-85937-920-6

Paperback Edition 2004
ISBN 1-85937-663-0

British Library Cataloguing in Publication Data

Francis Frith's Wellingborough Living Memories
Martin Andrew

Frith Book Company Ltd
Frith's Barn, Teffont,
Salisbury, Wiltshire SP3 5QP
Tel: +44 (0) 1722 716 376
Email: info@francisfrith.co.uk
www.francisfrith.co.uk

Printed and bound in Great Britain

Front Cover: **MIDLAND ROAD** *c1950* w279025
Frontispiece: **SILVER STREET** *c1950* W279008

The colour-tinting is for illustrative purposes only, and is not intended to be historically accurate

AS WITH ANY HISTORICAL DATABASE THE FRITH ARCHIVE IS CONSTANTLY BEING CORRECTED AND IMPROVED, AND THE PUBLISHERS WOULD WELCOME INFORMATION ON OMISSIONS OR INACCURACIES

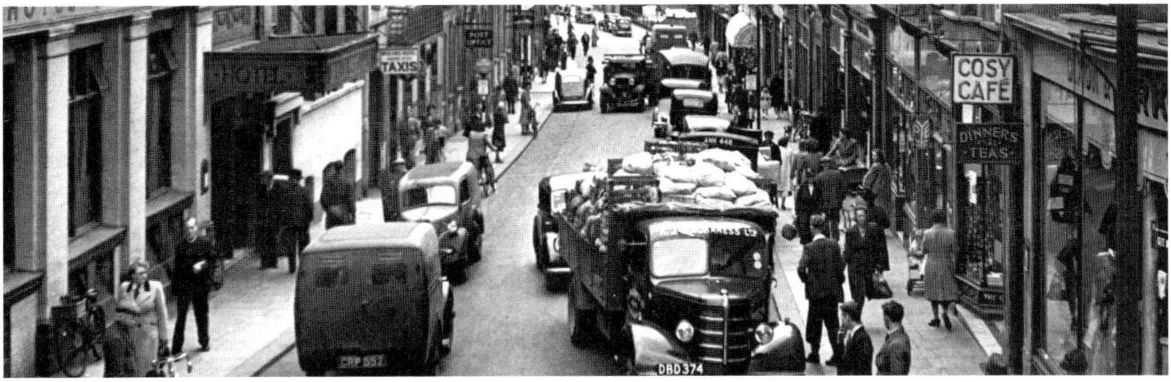

CONTENTS

FRANCIS FRITH

VICTORIAN PIONEER

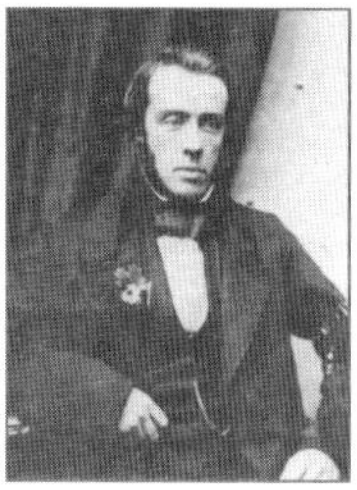

FRANCIS FRITH, founder of the world-famous photographic archive, was a complex and multi-talented man. A devout Quaker and a highly successful Victorian businessman, he was philosophical by nature and pioneering in outlook.

By 1855 he had already established a wholesale grocery business in Liverpool, and sold it for the astonishing sum of £200,000, which is the equivalent today of over £15,000,000. Now a very rich man, he was able to indulge his passion for travel. As a child he had pored over travel books written by early explorers, and his fancy and imagination had been stirred by family holidays to the sublime mountain regions of Wales and Scotland. 'What lands of spirit-stirring and enriching scenes and places!' he had written. He was to return to these scenes of grandeur in later years to 'recapture the thousands of vivid and tender memories', but with a different purpose. Now in his thirties, and captivated by the new science of photography, Frith set out on a series of pioneering journeys up the Nile and to the Near East that occupied him from 1856 unti 1860.

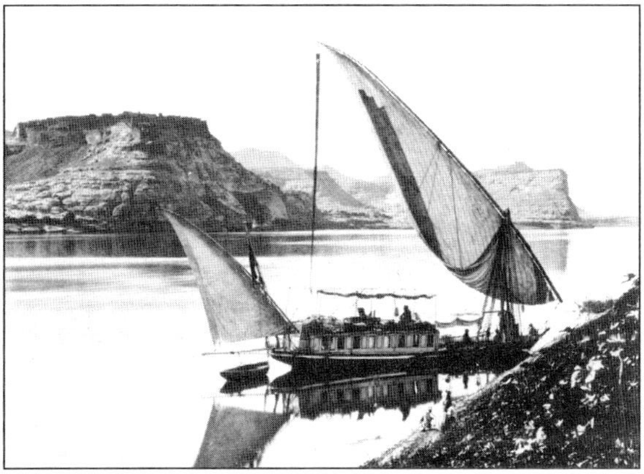

INTRIGUE AND EXPLORATION

These far-flung journeys were packed with intrigue and adventure. In his life story, written when he was sixty-three, Frith tells of being held captive by bandits, and of fighting 'an awful midnight battle to the very point of surrender with a deadly pack of hungry, wild dogs'. Wearing flowing Arab costume, Frith arrived at Akaba by camel sixty years before Lawrence of Arabia, where he encountered 'desert princes and rival sheikhs, blazing with jewel-hilted swords'.

He was the first photographer to venture beyond the sixth cataract of the Nile. Africa was still the mysterious 'Dark Continent', and Stanley and Livingstone's historic meeting was a decade into the future. The conditions for picture taking confound belief. He laboured for hours in his wicker dark-room in the sweltering heat of the desert, while the volatile chemicals fizzed dangerously in their trays. Back in London he exhibited his photographs and was 'rapturously cheered' by members of the Royal Society. His reputation as a photographer was made overnight.

VENTURE OF A LIFE-TIME

Characteristically, Frith quickly spotted the opportunity to create a new business as a specialist publisher of photographs. He lived in an era of immense and sometimes violent change. For the poor in the early part of Victoria's reign work was exhausting and the hours long, and people had precious little free time to enjoy themselves. Most people had no transport other than a cart or gig at their disposal, and rarely

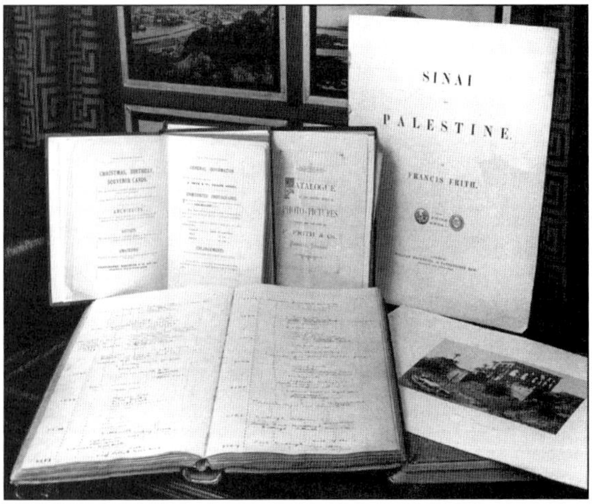

travelled far beyond the boundaries of their own town or village. However, by the 1870s the railways had threaded their way across the country, and Bank Holidays and half-day Saturdays had been made obligatory by Act of Parliament. All of a sudden the working man and his family were able to enjoy days out and see a little more of the world.

With typical business acumen, Francis Frith foresaw that these new tourists would enjoy having souvenirs to commemorate their days out. In 1860 he married Mary Ann Rosling and set out on a new career: his aim was to photograph every city, town and village in Britain. For the next thirty years he travelled the country by train and by pony and trap, producing fine photographs of seaside resorts and beauty spots that were keenly bought by millions of Victorians. These prints were painstakingly pasted into family albums and pored over during the dark nights of winter, rekindling precious memories of summer excursions.

THE RISE OF FRITH & CO

Frith's studio was soon supplying retail shops all over the country. To meet the demand he gathered about him a small team of photographers, and published the work of independent artist-photographers of the calibre of Roger Fenton and Francis Bedford. In order to gain some understanding of the scale of Frith's business one only has to look at the catalogue issued by Frith & Co in 1886: it runs to some 670 pages, listing not only many thousands of views of the British Isles but also many photographs of most European countries, and China, Japan, the USA and Canada - note the sample page shown on page 9 from the hand-written Frith & Co ledgers recording the pictures. By 1890 Frith had created the greatest specialist photographic publishing company in the world, with over 2,000 sales outlets - more than the combined number that Boots and WH Smith have today! The picture on the next page shows the Frith & Co display board at Ingleton in the Yorkshire Dales (left of window). Beautifully constructed with a mahogany frame and gilt inserts, it could display up to a dozen local scenes.

POSTCARD BONANZA

The ever-popular holiday postcard we know today took many years to develop. In 1870 the Post Office issued the first plain cards, with a pre-printed stamp on one face. In 1894 they allowed other publishers' cards to be sent through the mail with an attached adhesive halfpenny stamp. Demand grew rapidly, and in 1895 a new size of postcard was permitted called the court card, but there was little room for illustration. In 1899, a year after Frith's death, a new card measuring 5.5 x 3.5 inches became the standard format, but it was not until 1902 that the divided back came into being, so that the address and message could be on one face and a full-size illustration on the other. Frith & Co were in the vanguard of postcard development: Frith's sons Eustace and Cyril continued their father's monumental task, expanding the number of views offered to the public and recording more and more places in Britain, as the coasts and countryside were opened up to mass travel.

Francis Frith had died in 1898 at his villa in Cannes, his great project still growing. The archive he created continued in business for another seventy years. By 1970 it contained over a third of a million pictures showing 7,000 British towns and villages.

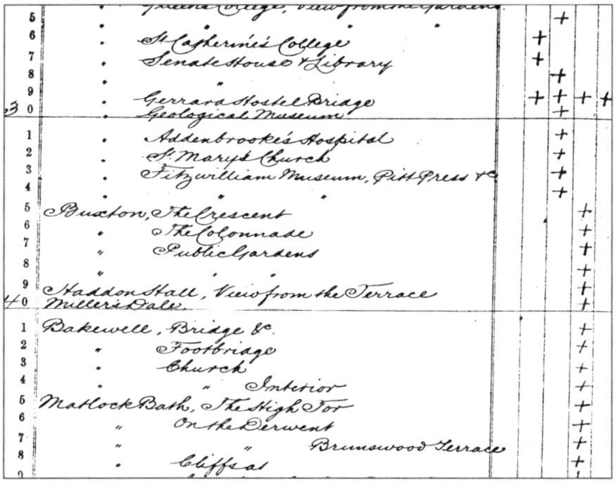

6 St Catherine's College
7 Senate House & Library
8
9 Gerrard Hostel Bridge
30 Geological Museum
1 Addenbrooke's Hospital
2 St Mary's Church
3 Fitzwilliam Museum, Pitt Press &c
4
5 Buxton, The Crescent
6 The Colonnade
7 Public Gardens
8
9 Haddon Hall, View from the Terrace
40 Millers Dale
1 Bakewell, Bridge &c.
2 Footbridge
3 Church
4 Interior
5 Matlock Bath, The High Tor
6 On the Derwent
7 Brunswood Terrace
8 Cliffs at

FRANCIS FRITH'S LEGACY

Frith's legacy to us today is of immense significance and value, for the magnificent archive of evocative photographs he created provides a unique record of change in the cities, towns and villages throughout Britain over a century and more. Frith and his fellow studio photographers revisited locations many times down the years to update their views, compiling for us an enthralling and colourful pageant of British life and character.

We are fortunate that Frith was dedicated to recording the minutiae of everyday life. For it is this sheer wealth of visual data, the painstaking chronicle of changes in dress, transport, street layouts, buildings, housing, engineering and landscape that captivates us so much today. His remarkable images offer us a powerful link with the past and with the lives of our ancestors.

THE VALUE OF THE ARCHIVE TODAY

Computers have now made it possible for Frith's many thousands of images to be accessed almost instantly. Frith's images are increasingly used as visual resources, by social historians, by researchers into genealogy and ancestry, by architects and town planners, and by teachers involved in local history projects.

In addition, the archive offers every one of us an opportunity to examine the places where we and our families have lived and worked down the years. Highly successful in Frith's own era, the archive is now, a century and more on, entering a new phase of popularity. Historians consider the Francis Frith Collection to be of prime national importance. It is the only archive of its kind remaining in private ownership. Francis Frith's archive is now housed in an historic timber barn in the beautiful village of Teffont in Wiltshire. Its founder would not recognize the archive office as it is today. In place of the many thousands of dusty boxes containing glass plate negatives and an all-pervading odour of photographic chemicals, there are now ranks of computer screens. He would be amazed to watch his images travelling round the world at unimaginable speeds through internet lines.

The archive's future is both bright and exciting. Francis Frith, with his unshakeable belief in making photographs available to the greatest number of people, would undoubtedly approve of what is being done today with his lifetime's work. His photographs depicting our shared past are now bringing pleasure and enlightenment to millions around the world a century and more after his death.

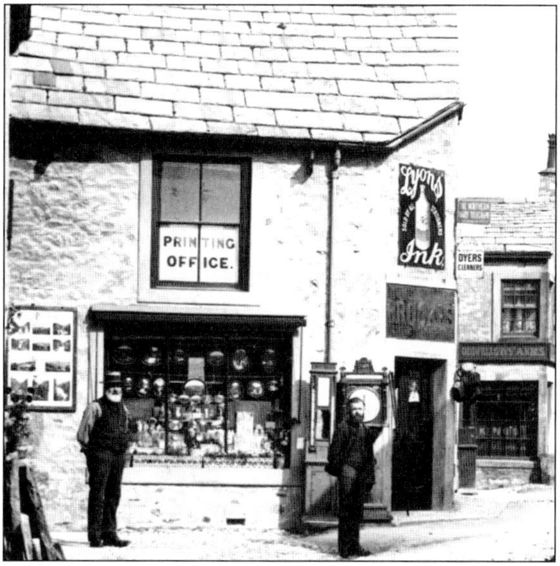

WELLINGBOROUGH

AN INTRODUCTION

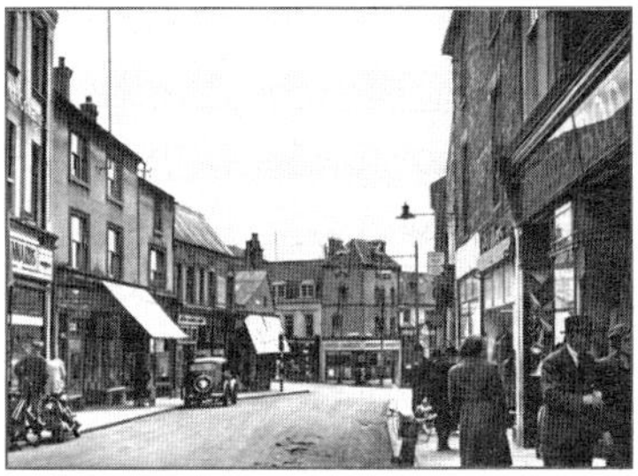

WELLINGBOROUGH, an ancient market town set on higher ground above the valley of the River Nene, grew up at the crossroads of two major routes. However, since the building of the A45 dual carriageway from the M1 as far as Rushden in the 1980s, the east-west route has by-passed the town. Nevertheless, it seems just as busy in traffic terms today, despite the fact that the A509 now also bypasses Wellingborough in a ring road, skirting its westward expansion and passing between this and the giant Park Farm industrial estate.

Although this book is in the 'Living Memories' series, concentrating on the town as it was between the 1940s and the 1960s, a few words on the town's history is necessary to provide a context. Granted to Croyland Abbey in Lincolnshire by King Eadred in AD948, Wellingborough continued to be owned by the abbot and his monks until Croyland Abbey was dissolved under Henry VIII in 1539. The abbots had secured a market charter from King John in 1201 which authorised a weekly market to be held every Wednesday. Henry VI also granted a charter to the abbot in 1447 allowing him to hold two annual fairs. Thus the market town grew up supervised by the monks of Croyland Abbey. Remnants of their grange house

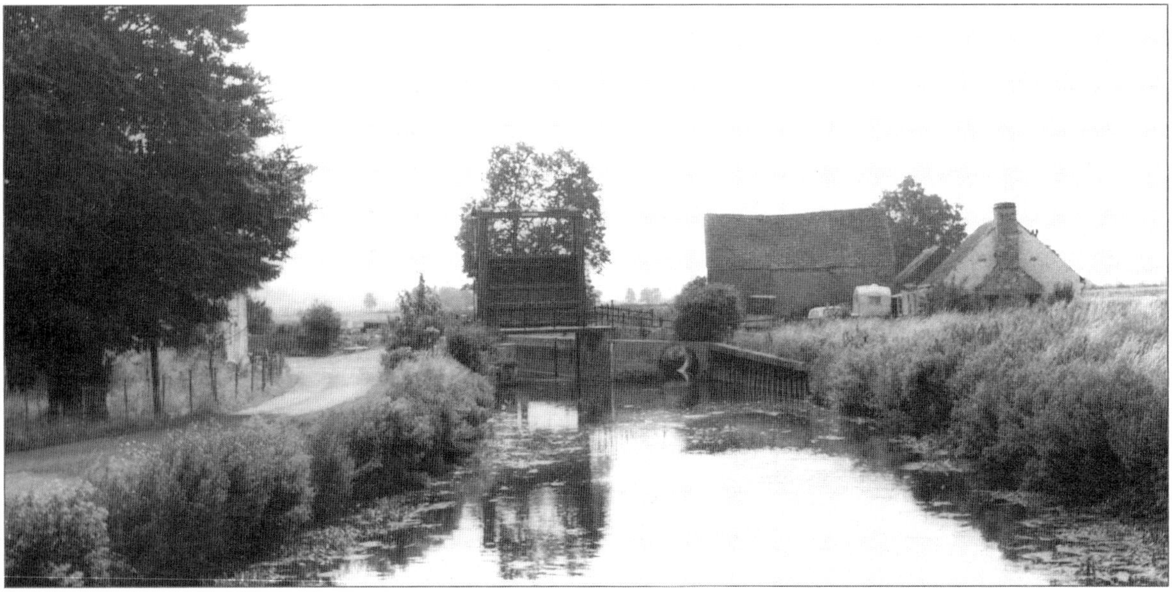

GREAT DODDINGTON, *The River Nene c1960* G137010

are buried within the present Croyland Hall, while their tithe barn has survived and has been restored - the work started within the time-span of this book. After the Dissolution, the manor passed to Princess Elizabeth, later Queen Elizabeth I, who divided it up. The market rights went to Sir Nicholas Hatton, her mighty courtier, who built Holdenby House and Kirby Hall in Northamptonshire.

The subsequent history in this introduction is intended to show how the town in the form it had reached by World War II evolved and changed in the 1950s and 1960s. We must remember that all this change was taking place in an historic market town context. The skeleton of the old town breaks through all over, and in many places it is still clothed with the flesh of medieval, Tudor, Stuart, Georgian and Victorian fabric. The past is still very much present in the town's plan and architecture, despite the ravages it has suffered in the cause of regeneration and revival. One could feel that things would have been done differently now: in particular, a key former civic building such as the Corn Exchange might not be demolished, and the wholesale destruction between Sheep Street and Midland Road might not take place.

This book uses photographs of the town and its surroundings taken in the 1950s and 1960s, and captures the town just as its status as a post-Second World War London overspill town began to bear fruit. In 1962 the corporation signed a new agreement with the Greater London Council, successor to the London County Council, and development accelerated greatly. The old industries (boot and shoe making, brewing, and ironstone quarrying and foundries), the previous economic base of the town, were in effect replaced by a ring of industrial estates. The Denington Estate, for example, south of the town, was completed and fully occupied by 1967. London Overspill, a step down from New Town status, changed the demographics of Wellingborough, with influxes of Londoners diluting the Northamptonshire blood; they were followed by Asian, West Indian and Polish residents. Now the Christian churches, ranging from the medieval parish church to a Friends Meeting House, have been augmented by a golden-domed Hindu temple in Highfield Road and a mosque in Strode Road, for example.

From having a population of around 18,000 in 1901 Wellingborough has grown to around 40,000 today (considerably fewer than the 83,000 projected in the development plan). In 1945 the town was still fairly compact. It had expanded in Victorian times, mainly eastwards towards the Midland Railway and northwards to a similar extent. The inter-war years saw continued expansion around the fringes, including estates off Croyland Road, newly built in 1929. However, the most spectacular swallowing of the countryside took place from the 1950s on, mainly to the west and north. Now Wellingborough and its suburbs have a diameter of about 3 miles, with major industrial estates on the fringes. The London Overspill phase is over, of course, but the town centre survived relatively intact until the 1960s, apart from the odd World War II bomb and some local rebuilding.

For those of us who remember Wellingborough in the early 1960s, the somewhat run-down but characterful market town has been transformed by redevelopment, which took place mostly in a period when developers and eager councillors saw demolition and rebuilding as the only way to regenerate sleepy, decaying towns. In the captions there is frequent reference to the impact of the

Swansgate Shopping Centre, built as an Arndale Centre. (Was any town free of such history-careless shopping malls at this time)? Constructed in 1974, it involved the demolition of a key section of the historic town in a block bounded by Sheep Street, Market Street, Midland Road and Commercial Lane, then a narrow lane. Within this area there used to be an ancient lane, Cheese Lane; the Lyric cinema; Praed's Brewery; and numerous buildings on a human scale. A few survived to front Sheep Street and Market Street, but the effect was to destroy Midland Road as one of the principal shopping streets in the town.

The Arndale Centre with its inward-looking covered shopping streets was opened in June 1977 by the Duke of Gloucester. While covered shopping is convenient, it produces lifeless outer elevations and out-of-scale architecture. The worst offence this building committed, though, is the seven-storey office tower that dominates views up Sheep Street. The Arndale Centre was refurbished in the late 1980s, and the name was changed to Swansgate (in deference, no doubt, to the Swan Brewery which it supplanted, and to the medieval abbot's swannery). Inside, one of the four main malls commemorates Cheese Lane, and the terra cotta swan plaque from Dulley's Brewery building has been reset at the mall crossroads: a sop to the past.

To me, while it was understandable at the time, the Swansgate Shopping Centre is perhaps the most damaging development that took place as far as impact on the historic town goes. However, at the same time as the site clearances and whole-sale demolitions for the Arndale Centre were under way, there were more positive signs of respect for the past. The 15th-century tithe barn, a link with medieval Wellingborough, was finally repaired and brought into community use - it survived the setback of a major fire in 1972 which virtually destroyed the roof.

Much of what is seen in this book has survived, but equally much has gone since the 1960s. The Zoo Park closed around 1970, and most of its site is now occupied by offices and car parks grouped around Tithe Barn Road. One office building, the former National Farmers Union block, dominates the setting of the tithe barn and Croyland Hall. The latter has been rescued and repaired; it now houses the Wellingborough Borough Council's planning department and the Wellingborough Heritage Centre.

The Corn Exchange, built in 1861 and latterly a cinema, was demolished in 1959, completing the vandalism that the Luftwaffe had begun when a Dornier dropped bombs on the Market Square area in August 1942. In Chapter 3, two successive views show the scene with the Corn Exchange there and then with it vanished (W279049 in c1955 and W279060 in c1965 both on page 38). These photographs also show buildings with corrugated iron roofs - these just about survived the bomb, but were later swept away. The area east of the market place was also cleared as far east as Pebble Lane, to be replaced by characterless modern buildings.

The net effect of the redevelopments, well-intentioned no doubt, was severely to damage the spirit of place of the town centre, and literally to knock the stuffing out of the town's core. No amount of worthy pedestrianisation schemes can recompense for the loss of buildings that together shape the character and appearance of a town. In recent years the council has worked hard to improve the quality of the town centre; besides pedestrianising part of Market Street and the market place, it has laid red paviours in Cambridge Street, the rest of Market Street and down Midland Road.

Some of the developments seen in this book are now assuming the respectability of age. The Technical College in Church Street, now part of Tresham College (it replaced a smaller brick Victorian Technical Institute in the 1960s) is an interesting building of its period; so is the Borough Council offices building between Croyland Hall and the Swanspool Brook, its four and five storeys clad in areas of blue Westmoreland slate. Perhaps these buildings and others will one day come to be seen as a vital part of the town's heritage. Whatever one thinks now, they at least and others like them were carefully designed - unlike some of the drab cheap stuff thrown up in the town centre (in view W279059 next to the Ford Zodiac, for instance on page 17). Also on the positive side, the tawdry Fine Fare supermarket building that succeeded the Corn Exchange had its own nemesis when it was demolished in 1995. Other buildings are less easy to forgive, such as the Telephone Exchange in Midland Road: its five slab-sided storeys are an ugly intrusion into the townscape.

Other losses include the Zoo Park, which flourished from 1943, was extended in 1957, and finally closed in about 1970; it is probably no real loss, as zoos have moved on from big cats and polar bears in smallish cages. The open-air swimming pool also enjoyed a heyday in the 1950s, but tastes have changed: covered pools and leisure centres are needed for this richer, more pampered and leisure-orientated day

The views in this book also capture Wellingborough (and many of the other towns and villages in the last two chapters) at the end of the period of the economic dominance of the boot and shoe manufacturing industry. This is rich agricultural and grazing country, so there was a ready supply of hides for leather making; Wellingborough had a local cottage industry of shoe making from the mid-18th century onwards. Lace making also flourished, declining after the 1820s; but boot and shoe making expanded very rapidly to dominate the town's economy, particularly after the railway arrived. The first line was a branch line linking Northampton and Peterborough. The station opened in 1845, while a further station followed in 1858 actually on the main London Midland line. Midland Road was laid out in 1860 to connect this new station to the town centre.

By 1901 well over 2,000 people were employed in the boot and shoe trade. Many worked from workshops that employed about twenty hands dotted all over the town and its Victorian suburbs, while others worked in larger ones such as Yorke & Company in Oxford Street, which employed over a hundred hands. By 1970 the writing was on the wall, and the industry declined rapidly, unable to compete with cheap foreign imports and the great increase in demand for non-leather footwear.

The agricultural hinterland also fed the brewing industry in the town, but this folded up within the time-span of this book. Dulley's Brewery and Praed's Breweries were rivals and an important part of the town's economy, eventually merging and being taken over by Phipps of Northampton; Phipps themselves were absorbed by Watney Mann in 1960. Flour milling has been more successful - the Whitworth Brothers' giant mills on the Nene, the oldest of the three built in 1886, are a well-known landmark from the A45 and A609.

The iron smelting industry came to an end in 1962 with the closure of Wellingborough Iron Works on Finedon Road, the first foundry having opened here in 1886. In the new industrial estates many plots were taken by footwear manufacturers, including Sudborough & Wood, who relocated to the Denington Estate in 1964. Unfortunately this did not save them, and the factory was demolished in due course.

The town's economy is now much more diverse than it was in the 1950s, and there are far more facilities and shopping choice, but I cannot help feeling that the town portrayed in these views had more character. Certainly it did architecturally; but enough survives to give the town a sense of place. A comparison of the views in the book with the present day streetscape shows that many of the key buildings survive and continue to give shape to the town as an historic market town. These include Swanspool House and park, donated to the town in 1919, Ye Golden Lion, The Hind Hotel, Croyland Hall, the tithe barn, the parish church and the 17th-century former grammar school nearby. The main street plan survives - the town has lost only lanes and alleys. But it lacks a major public building from its glorious agrarian past: the Corn Exchange was demolished in 1959, and the Town Hall in Silver Street, erected in 1820, had been converted into shops by 1900 and is now The Red Well pub.

Many good buildings survive from later times, including the fine Georgian houses on the north side of Burystead Place, Leighton House, and other houses in the High Street and Broad Green. Odd 18th-century ironstone houses crop up in the town's streets, interspersed with the 19th- and early 20th-century buildings from the prosperous shoe-making years. The Victorian period added to the town's character greatly, with buildings as diverse as the 1875 Congregational church (now United Reformed) in view W279045 on page 31 and the banks in Market Street, such as Lloyds and the HSBC. The 20th century makes its contribution, including the Palace Theatre of 1911 and, far more importantly, Sir Ninian Comper's incomparable St Mary's church off Knox Road, started in 1906 and not completed until 1968. This grand ironstone and limestone church was mainly funded by the Sharman sisters, and its interior is quite outstanding. Comper was buried in Westminster Abbey, and was undoubtedly one of the country's finest church architects of the last century and a half; Wellingborough is lucky to have this masterpiece within its boundaries.

Despite the criticism of what has happened to the town in recent years, Wellingborough is a place I always enjoy visiting. I hope this collection of photographs from the 1950s and 1960s convinces you. If you already know the town or live here, I am sure you will agree that it has (and had) a lot to offer. These views show it before the worst mistake was made vis a vis its historic character: I refer, of course, to the Swansgate Shopping Centre.

SHEEP STREET SOUTHWARDS TO THE RIVER NENE

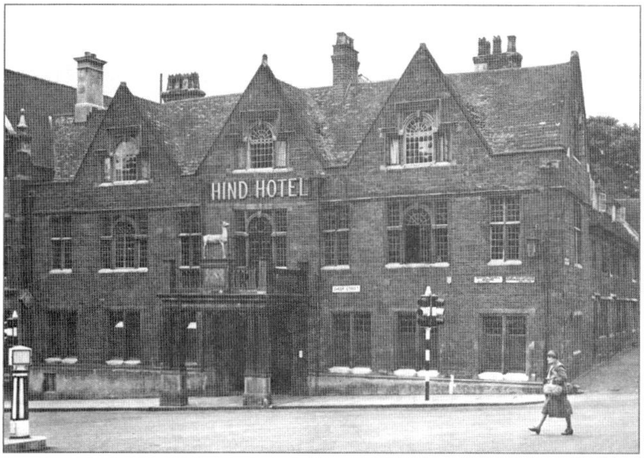

THE HIND HOTEL
c1950 W279009

Our tour of Wellingborough town is divided into three chapters which radiate north, east and south from the market place, where the view is terminated by the three gables of The Hind Hotel, one of the town's best older buildings and a former coaching inn. It dates from the 1640s and is built in the local russet ironstone with limestone dressings; its central carriageway was blocked and the timber porch built around 1900.

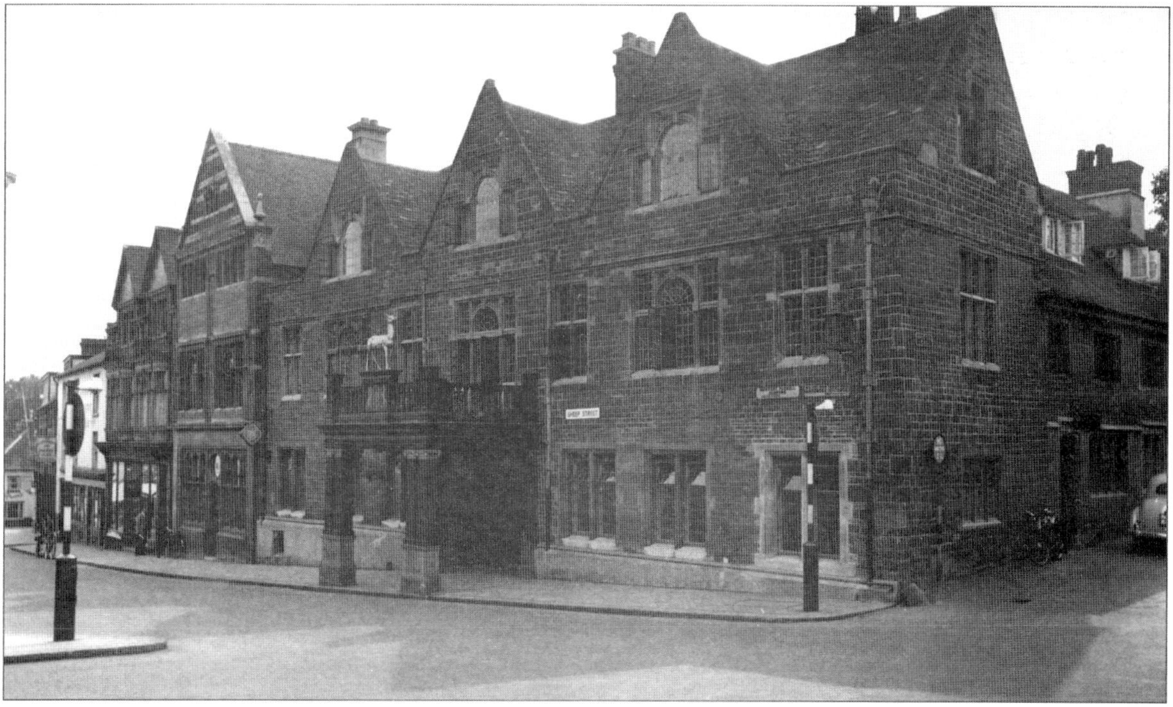

THE HIND HOTEL AND SHEEP STREET *c1955* W279050

Next to The Hind, down Sheep Street (left), is Oliver's coffee and tapas bar, the name presumably a reference to Oliver Cromwell, who may have stayed at The Hind in 1645 en route to the battle of Naseby. The building dates from 1902. The twin-gabled building to its left dates from 1886; it was formerly Wharton's bookshop but is now an estate agent's. The white building beyond is The Horseshoe Inn, which still retains a good 19th-century shopfront.

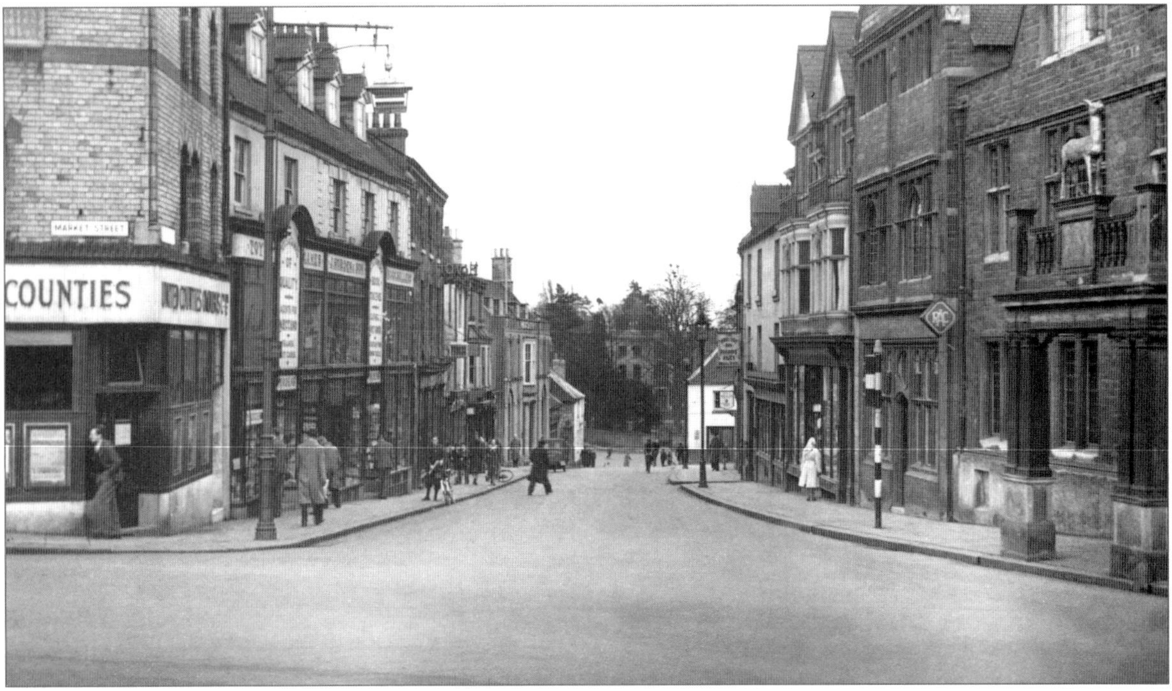

▲ **SHEEP STREET**
c1950 W279043

We are looking downhill towards Swanspool House. The building with the two-storey early 20th-century shopfront beyond the United Counties Omnibus Company (now Travel Care), was J Hordern & Son, a popular toyshop, booksellers and stationers; it closed in the 1960s, but the shopfront survives (although simplified). The buildings in the middle distance were demolished for the Arndale Centre, a vast shopping mall, now renamed the Swansgate Shopping Centre.

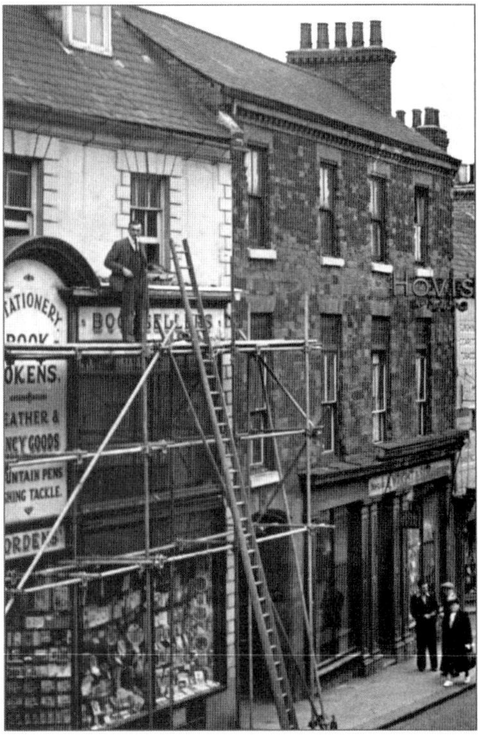

► **SHEEP STREET** *c1955* W279032a

Beyond the toyshop with its two-storeyed front, the somewhat patched brick building was a bakers and confectioners, Wright & Sons, demolished in the 1960s and replaced by a lower and unattractive building, now a solicitors. Hordern's in this view was undergoing refurbishment: the workman in his jacket stands casually with his thumbs in his waistcoat pocket - it was clearly a different era where safety was concerned.

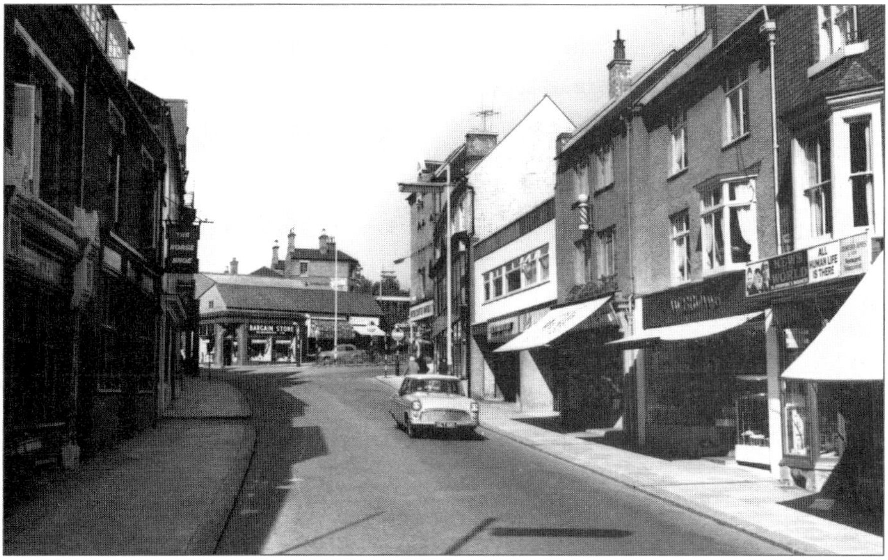

SHEEP STREET
c1965 W279059

The building that replaced the baker's has arrived (right). In the distance is Market Street, with buildings patched up after a World War II bomb fell here - they were subsequently demolished. The buildings on the left have lost their ornate shop fronts and are now a Yorkshire Bank. The road is not nowadays normally as free of traffic.

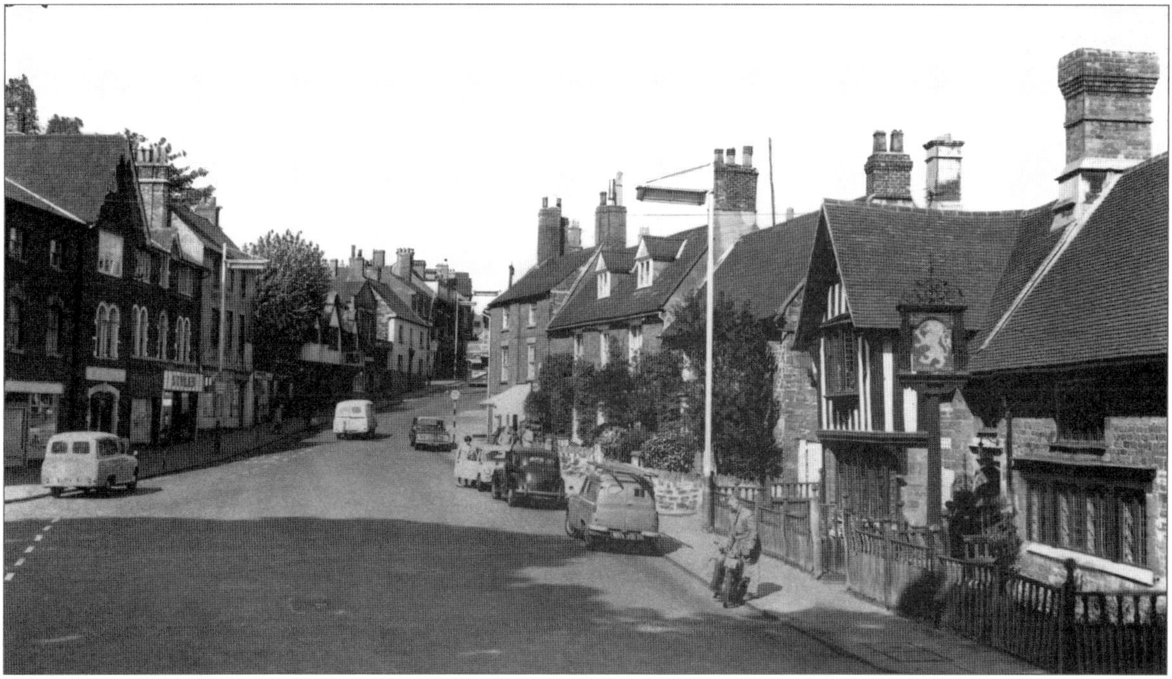

SHEEP STREET *c1965* W279058

This view from the foot of Sheep Street is now dominated on the right by the vast Swansgate Shopping Centre, opened in 1977, which swept away two of the town's breweries, Praed & Sons and Dulley's Swan Brewery - they later merged, and were then taken over by Phipps of Northampton. On the right is The Golden Lion, and on the left in the middle distance are the three thatched white gables belonging to the Tudor Restaurant, one of Wellingborough's oldest buildings and now a Chinese restaurant. To its left amid the trees was the entrance to the Zoo Park, the subject of the next two views.

THE ZOO PARK
c1965 W279074

Wellingborough's zoo opened in June 1943 during World War II in the grounds of Croyland Abbey. It was established by a Mr Stephens, who owned a pet shop in Midland Road, but it was formally opened by the chairman of the Urban District Council, Mr A Campbell, as a commemorative plaque informs us on the gate piers of the former entrance from Sheep Street.

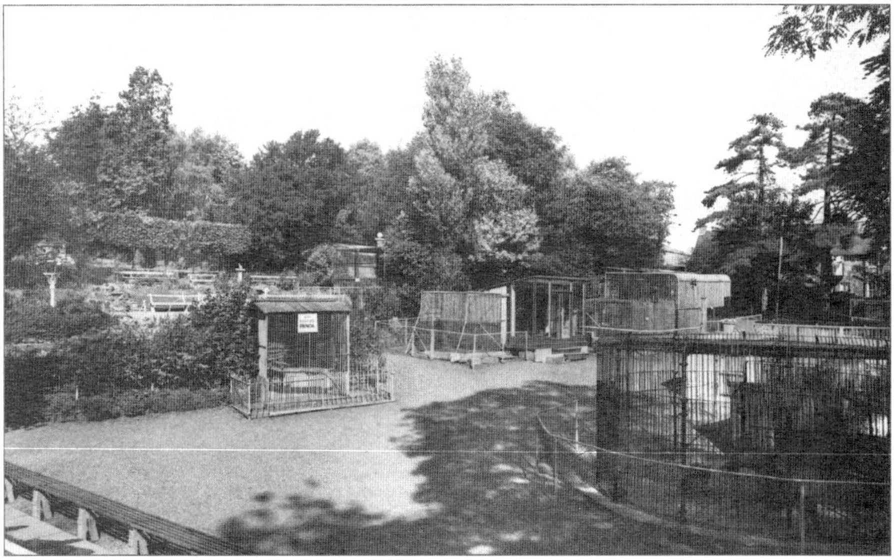

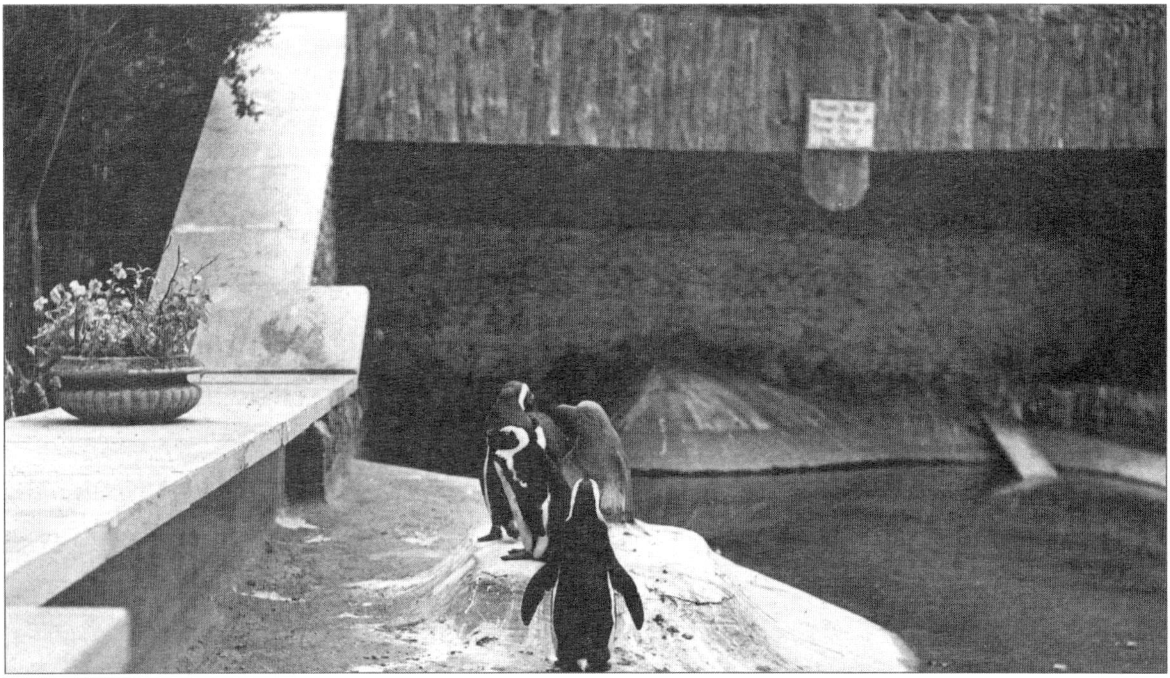

THE ZOO PARK, *The Penguins c1950* W279021

The zoo was a great success in its heyday, and expanded westwards in the 1950s along the banks of the Swanspool Brook, but changing fashions and more progressive thinking in zoological circles doomed such small local zoos, and it closed around 1970. This view is of the penguin pool; its animals also included elephants, lions (some of which were born here), tigers, and Blondie the polar bear, as well as water fowl such as black swans. The grounds reverted to parkland or were built over by office blocks.

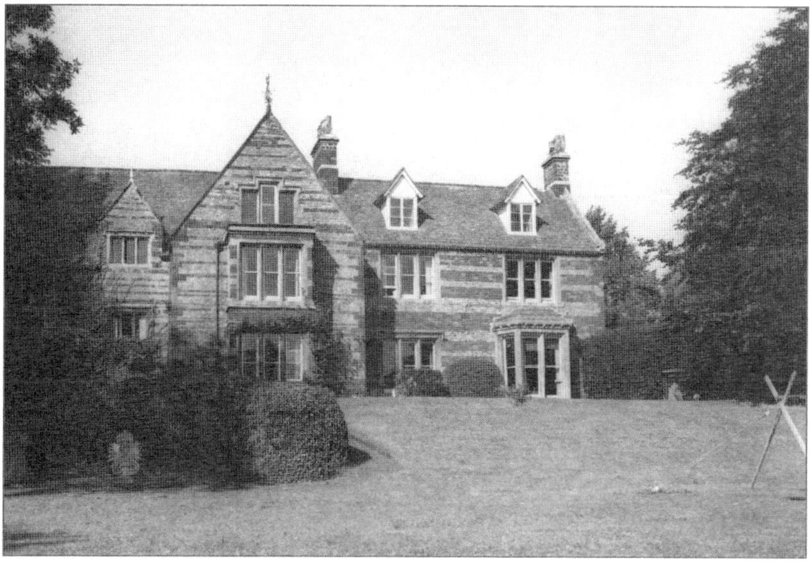

CROYLAND HALL
c1965 W279072

The zoo was formed within the grounds of Croyland Hall, on a site which is now at the end of Tithe Barn Road and flanked by dominating modern office blocks. Much of medieval Wellingborough was granted to Croyland Abbey in Lincolnshire in AD948 by King Eadred, and Croyland Hall occupies the site of their grange. Nearby the abbey's medieval tithe barn survives, well restored in the 1970s. Most of Croyland Hall post-dates the rule of the abbey: its earliest external walls are 17th-century, including the left-hand gables in this view, and the rest is Victorian.

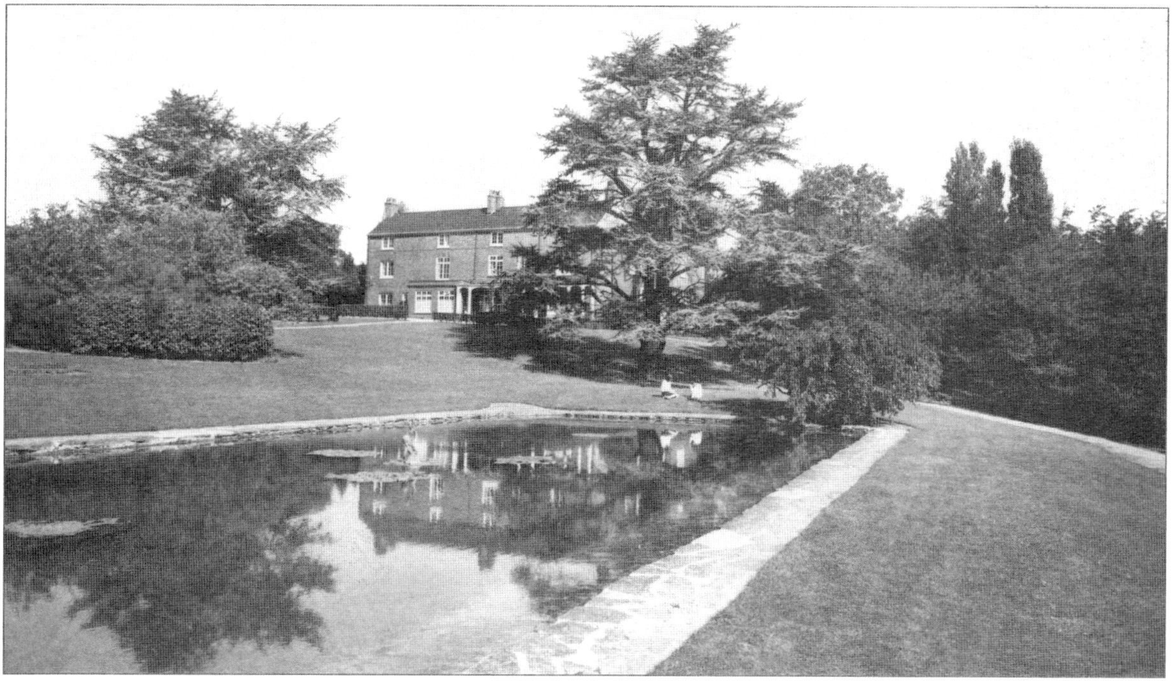

CROYLAND HALL GARDENS *c1965* W279083

This view looks from the grounds towards the west ranges of Croyland Hall - these are in brick, unlike the eastern ranges, which are in ironstone and white limestone. The pond has gone, but the right-hand cedar beyond survives. The left-hand cedar, partly obscured in the photograph, partially collapsed. Its trunk has been carved into a sculpture of swans to commemorate the medieval swannery of Croyland Abbey, which lay along the Swanspool Brook. To the left the view is now dominated by a 1974 office block.

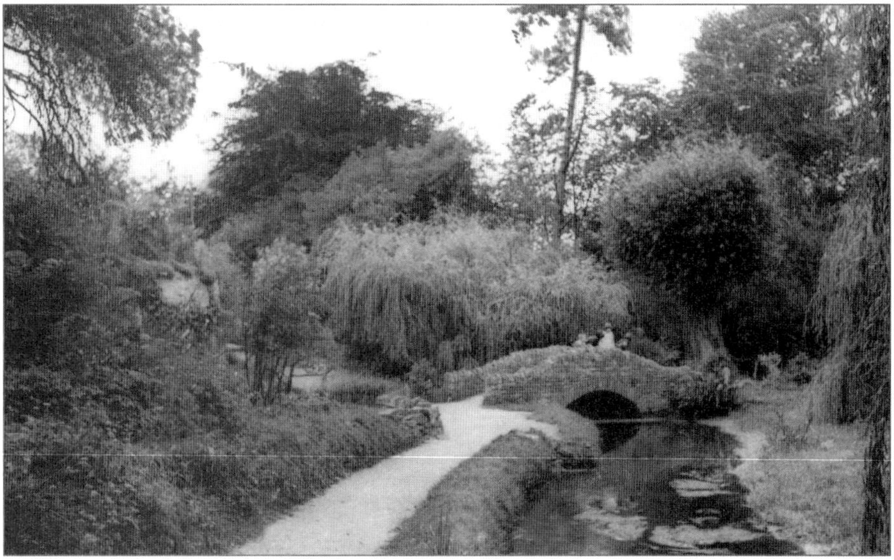

CROYLAND HALL GARDENS *c1965*
W279098

Further downhill, Frith's photographer looks east along the Swanspool Brook with its stone arched footbridge. The zoo lies beyond the trees in the distance. The stream's borders are now more informally landscaped, and an information board set up recently by Wellingborough Water Vole Watch informs us that the brook supports a thriving population of water voles.

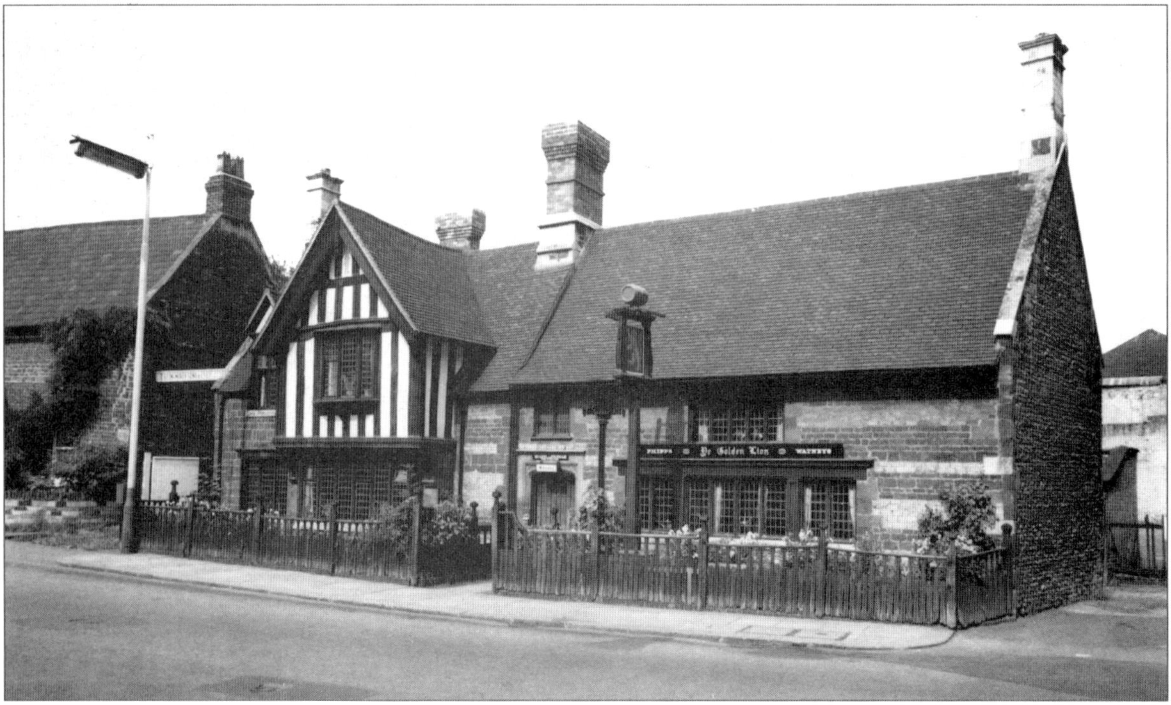

SHEEP STREET, *Ye Golden Lion c1965* W279123

Back in Sheep Street, this view is of another of Wellingborough's oldest buildings, Ye Golden Lion, which has a much restored timber-framed bay projecting from its ironstone and limestone-banded main range. Built as a house around 1540 and altered in the 17th century, it became an inn in 1830. Behind to the right are some of the buildings of Dulley's Brewery, now occupied by the multi-storey car park for the Swansgate Shopping Centre.

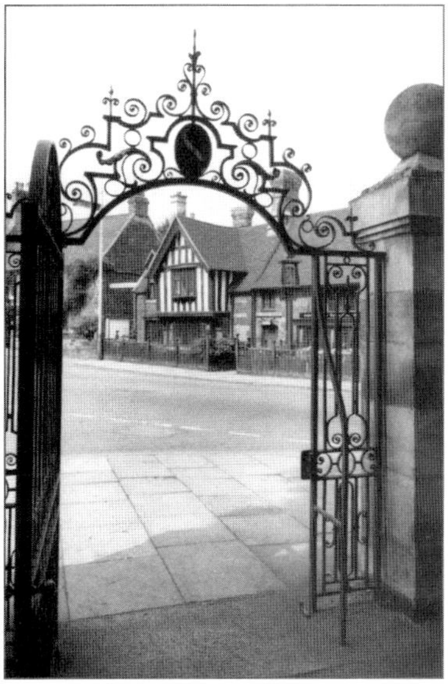

YE GOLDEN LION FROM SWANSPOOL HOUSE
c1965 W279122

Ye Golden Lion is seen here through the elegant wrought iron gates of Swanspool House with their overthrow and ball-finialled stone piers. Behind the photographer is the much travelled granite fountain. It was built in 1902 to commemorate King Edward VII's coronation, and originally stood in the market place until 1913; then it moved into the park, before coming finally to rest here. The former swan pool formed long ago by damming the Swanspool Brook separates the gateway from Swanspool House itself.

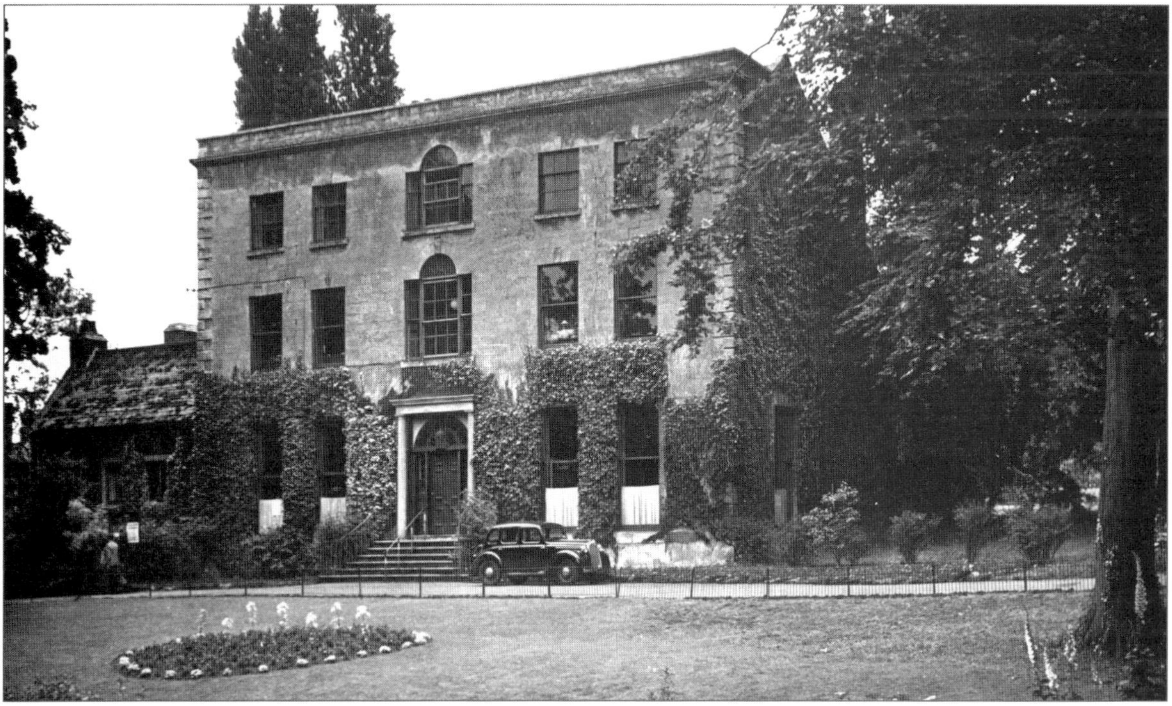

SWANSPOOL HOUSE *c1950* W279022

Swanspool House, built in 1778, closes the vista south down Sheep Street. An elegant stone house with central Venetian windows, it was presented to the town along with its grounds in 1919 by F C Chamberlain; it is now used as council offices, the council chamber and the register office, and forms the backdrop to many a wedding photograph. The foreground is now a car park. A sympathetic stone side porch was added in 1991.

▼ **SWANSPOOL GARDENS** *c1950* W279015

After 1919 the grounds became a public park with bowling greens and tennis courts. Although the grounds are now much municipalized, many of the 18th- and 19th-century trees survive. Swanspool House is behind the trees to the right, and on the left is a bronze statue of Euterpe, the Greek muse of music, with her lyre. Erected in 1932, it was stolen in the 1950s, and only the plinth now remains.

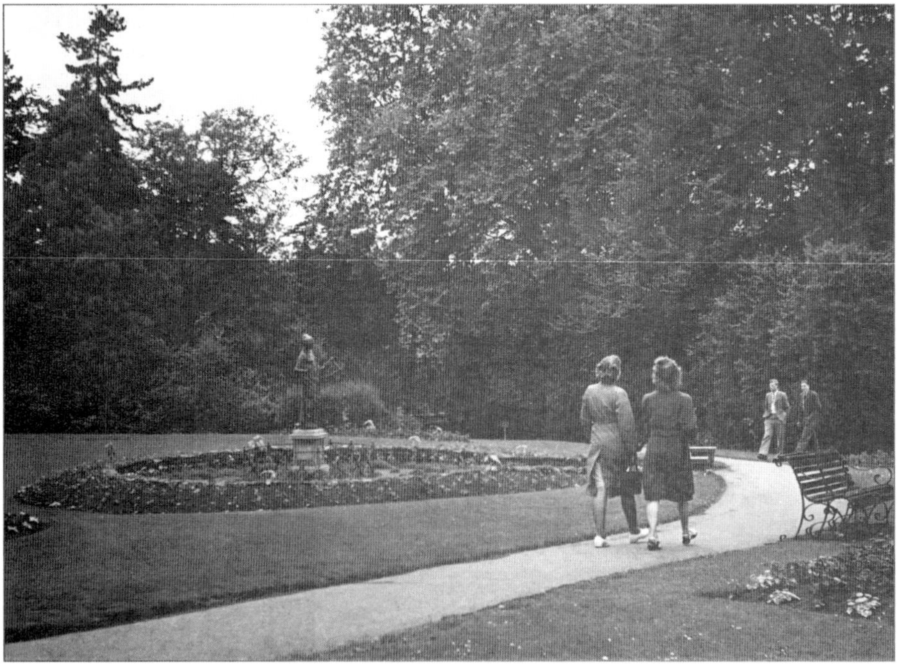

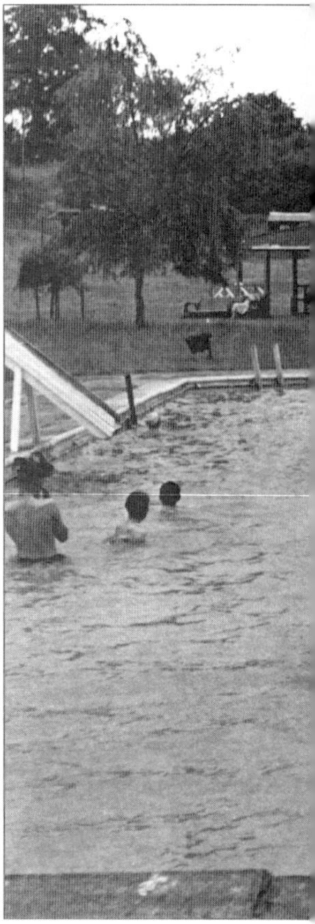

► **SWANSPOOL GARDENS** *c1950* W279014

Looking past the low walls on the right that surrounded the statue of Euterpe, we see some of the earliest trees from the park's pre-municipal days, and in the distance the raised platform of the bowling green with the 1930s houses of Swanspool Parade beyond. There are now fewer planted flower-beds, and the benches have gone or have been replaced, but the park remains a valuable asset to the town.

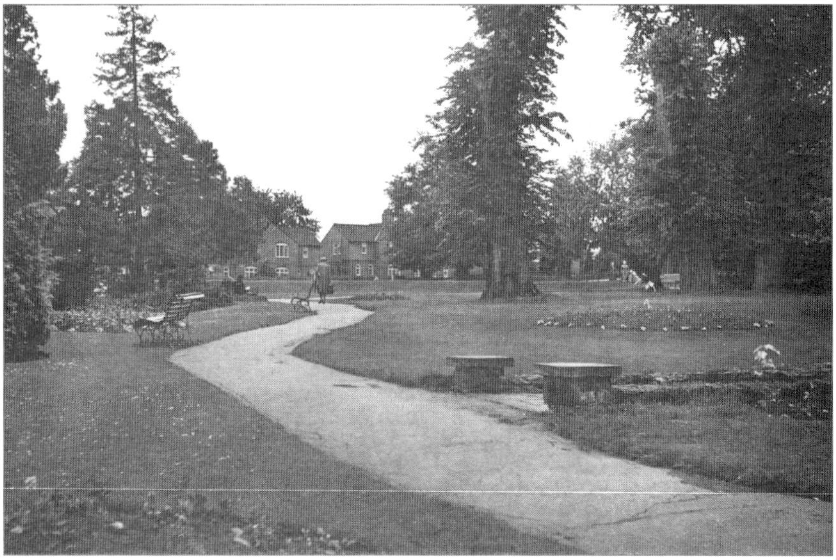

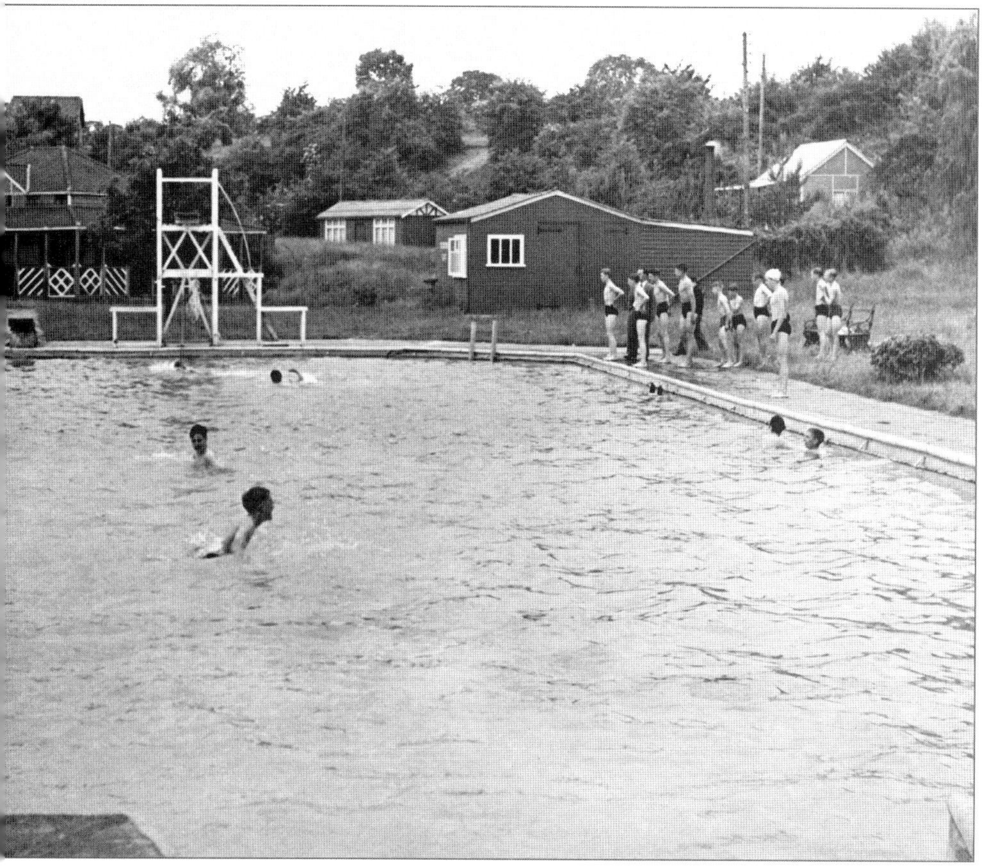

WILBY SWIMMING POOL *c1950*
W279013

In hardier days local swimming pools were open-air, and a popular theme for Frith photographers in the 1950s. Most are now replaced by heated indoor pools and leisure centres. Wellingborough's Wilby Lido was no exception, and this pool, built in former brick pits, was supplanted by the 1960s Wellingborough Swimming Pool off Croyland Road on the same site.

LONDON ROAD *c1965*
W279057

The London Road climbs southwards away from Sheep Street and the Swanspool Brook with good 18th- and 19th-century houses on the right, many behind walled front gardens. Just out of view to the right is the entrance to Castle Road. On the left the stone walls are those to Swanspool Park. The long building in the distance is the former Praed Brewery's mineral water factory, part of the brewery complex demolished in 1974.

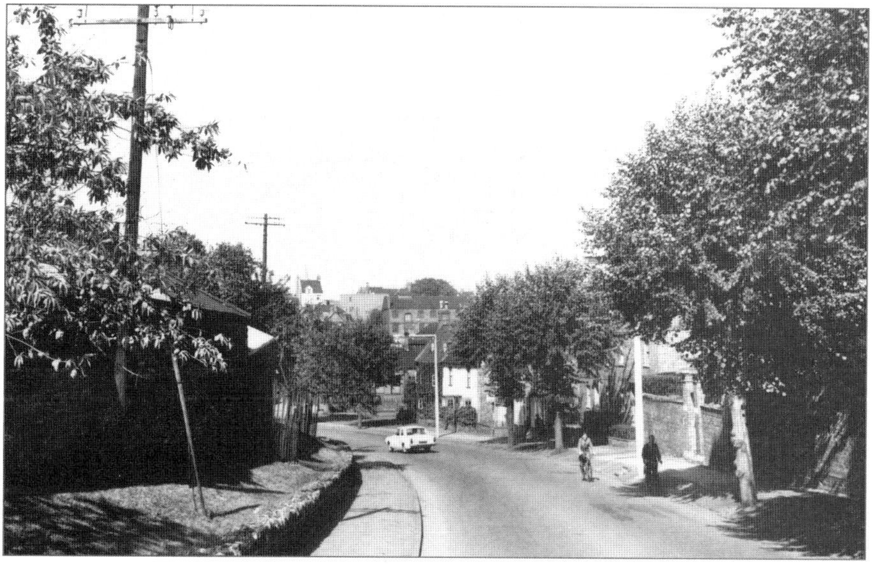

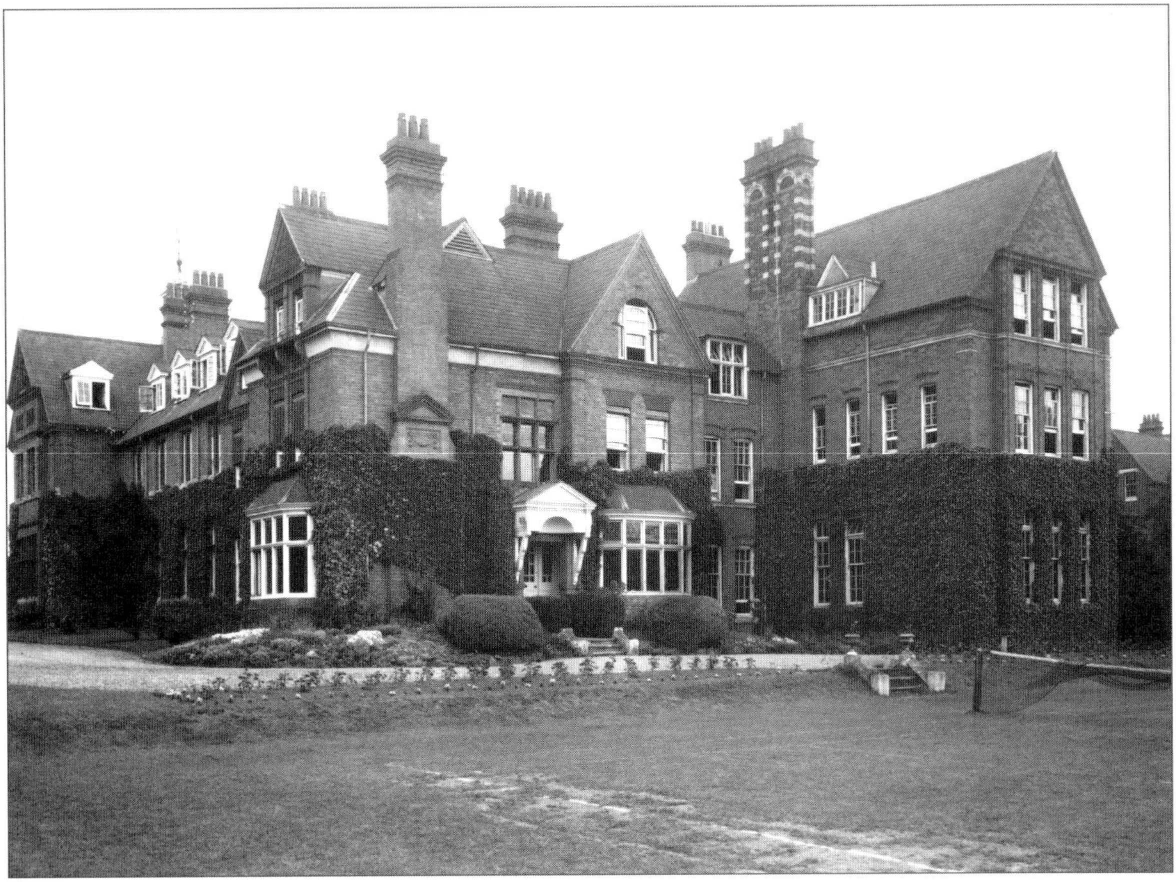

WELLINGBOROUGH SCHOOL
c1955 W279036

At the top of the hill on London Road is Wellingborough School, a co-educational public school that grew out of the town's Elizabethan grammar school founded in 1595, whose 1620 buildings survive on the north side of the parish churchyard. The school moved here in 1881 into buildings designed in Queen Anne/domestic revival style by Talbot Brown. The building on the left has a date plaque reading 'AD 1880', while the building on the far right was added in 1888. Since then many more buildings have been added as the school grows on its site, with playing fields stretching towards the River Nene.

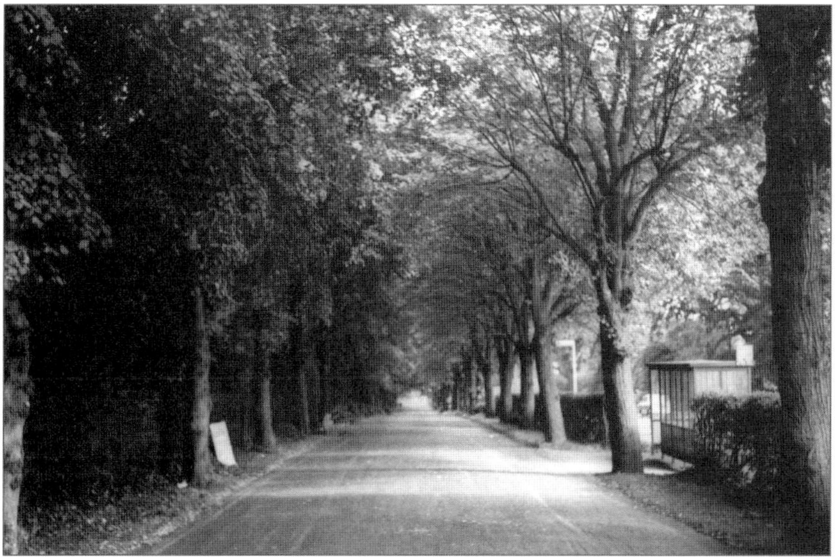

THE WALKS

London Road c1965 W279108

From beside Wellingborough School at the junction with Irthlingborough Road, a lime avenue runs for half a mile parallel to the busy London Road down to the banks of the River Nene. It was laid out as a pleasure promenade for the townspeople in the 1830s; it is remarkable that it has survived late 20th-century turbulence intact, except for a section where the Embankment roundabout cut a swathe through.

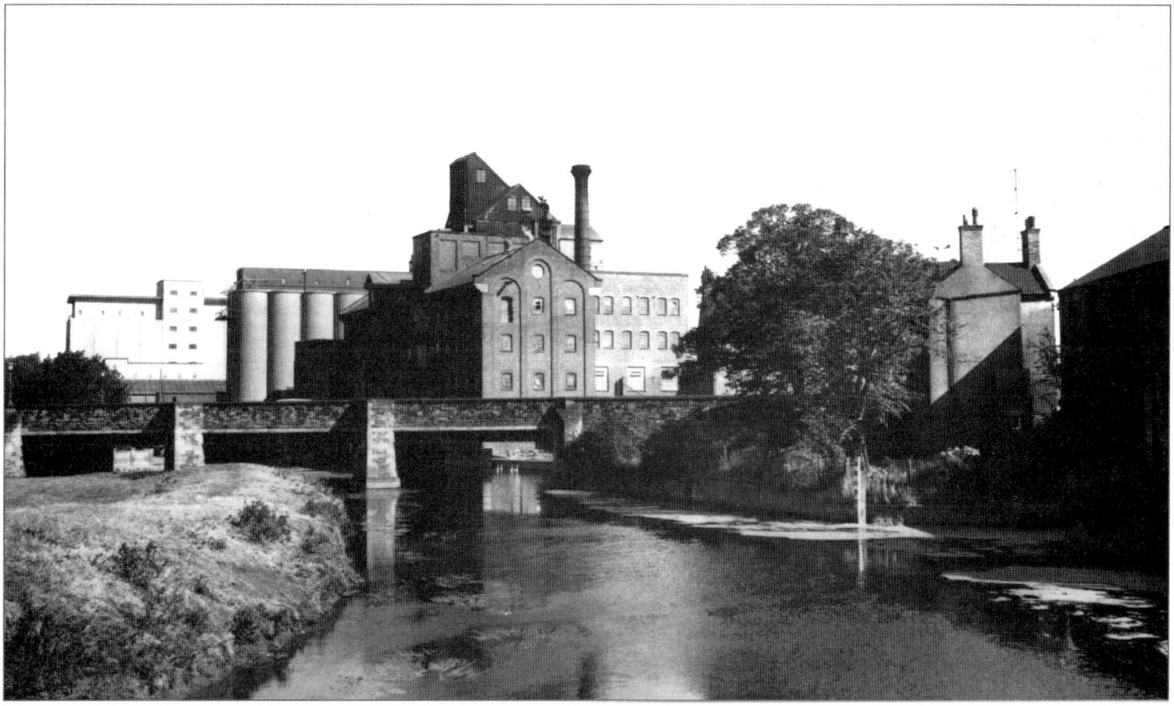

THE RIVER NENE AND VICTORIA MILLS *c1965* W279054

A well-known landmark to the south of the town, the Victoria Mills built by J B Whitworth for flour-milling in 1886 can now be seen from the A45 on its raised dual carriageway that now sweeps across the right-hand side of this view. The old tannery buildings on the right were demolished in 1980 to make way for the new highway. The bridge in front of the mills was rebuilt in 1980.

THE RIVER NENE
The Embankment c1965
W279056

This view looks east from the London Road bridge over the River Nene past the 1886 flour mill towards the vast 20th-century additional buildings added for Whitworth Brothers. In the foreground is the old barge wharf with the bag hoist gantry above, now removed. Grain still arrived by barge until about 1970, but it is now entirely brought in by road. The railway sidings have now also gone after the line closed to goods traffic in 1972.

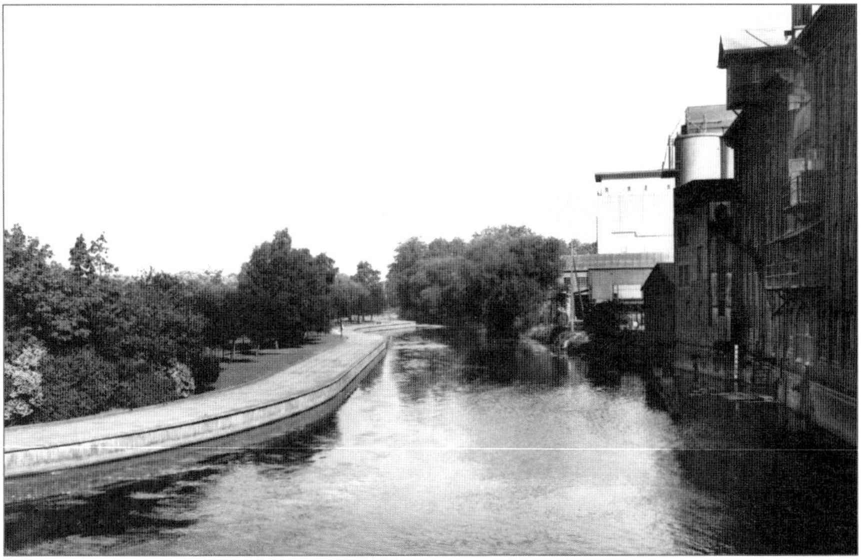

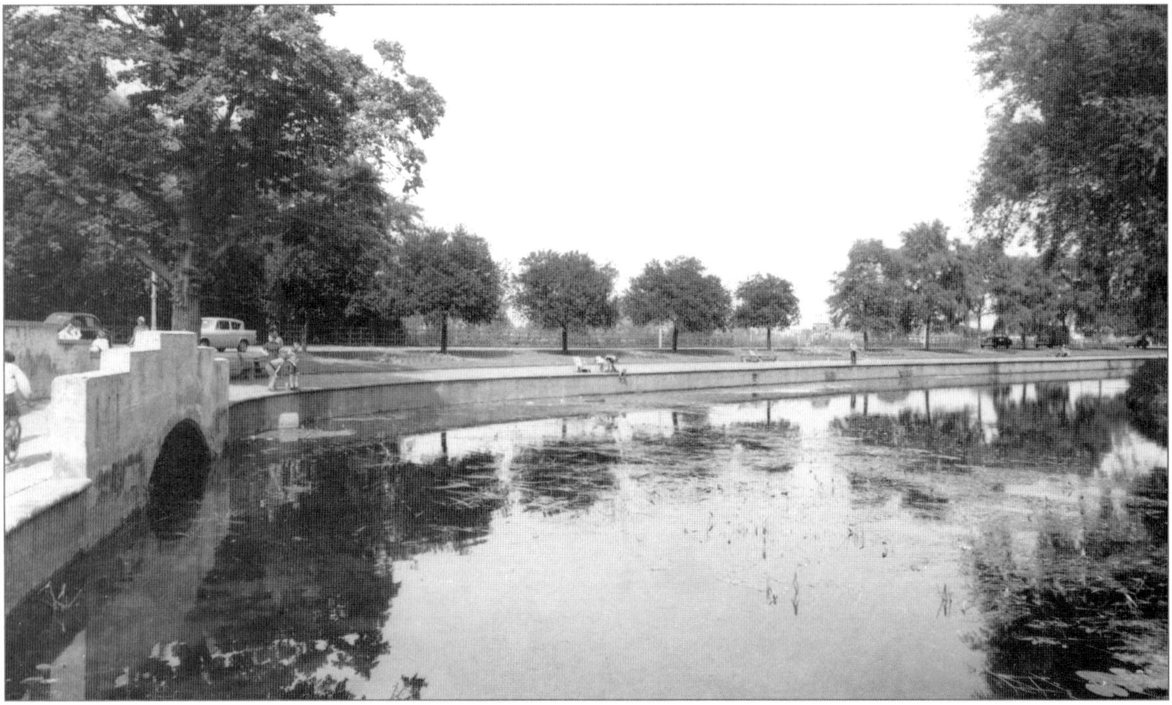

THE RIVER NENE, *The Embankment c1965* W279117

Opposite Victoria Mills the banks of the River Nene were turned into a riverside park: a broad riverside path was laid out, the park was landscaped, and a car park, public lavatories and a pond were built. This view looks north past the bridge that led from the pond. The parapets are now brick, and the pond is now empty and a roller-skating rink. Most of the park trees survive, and the river is popular with swans.

THE PARISH CHURCH AND SILVER STREET NORTHWARDS TO BROAD GREEN

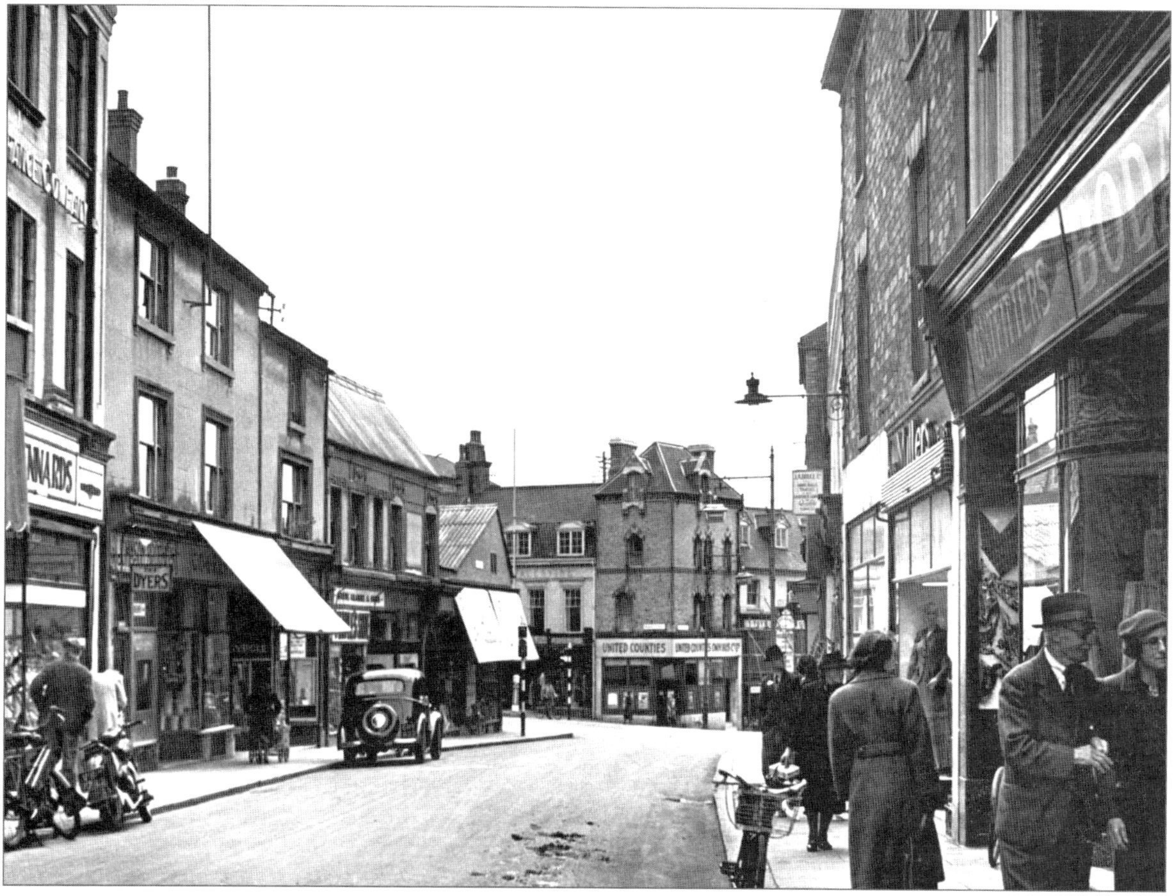

SILVER STREET
c1950 W279008

We now return to the Market Street junction. The second chapter heads north-west along Silver Street; in this view, though, we are looking back towards the Market Street junction, with the United Counties bus office on the corner. The two buildings beyond the car with temporary corrugated iron roofs (centre left) suffered serious bomb damage in a raid on August Bank Holiday 1942. The rather grand stone-fronted building on the left with the Ionic pilasters is now a charity shop.

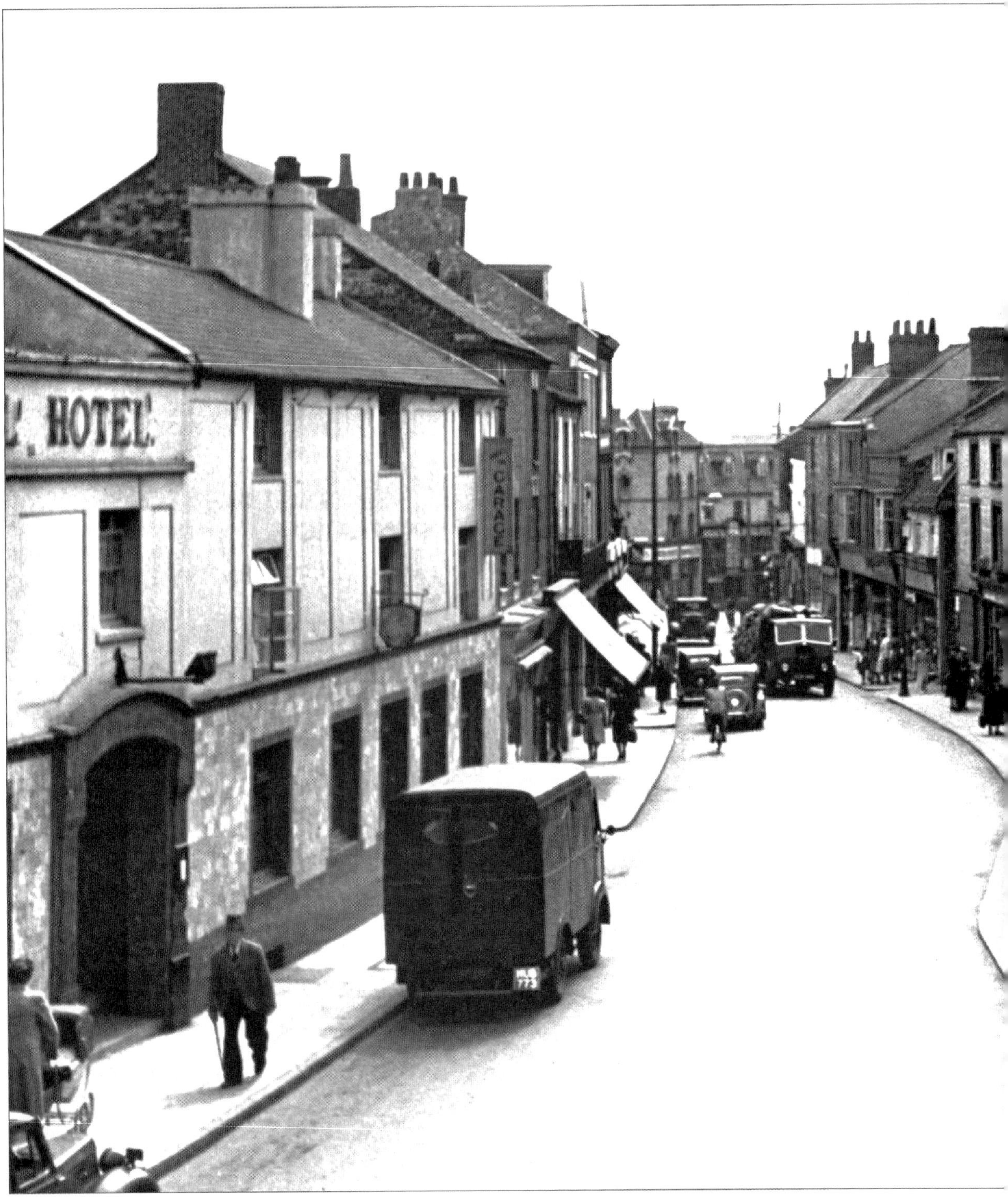
HOTEL
GARAGE

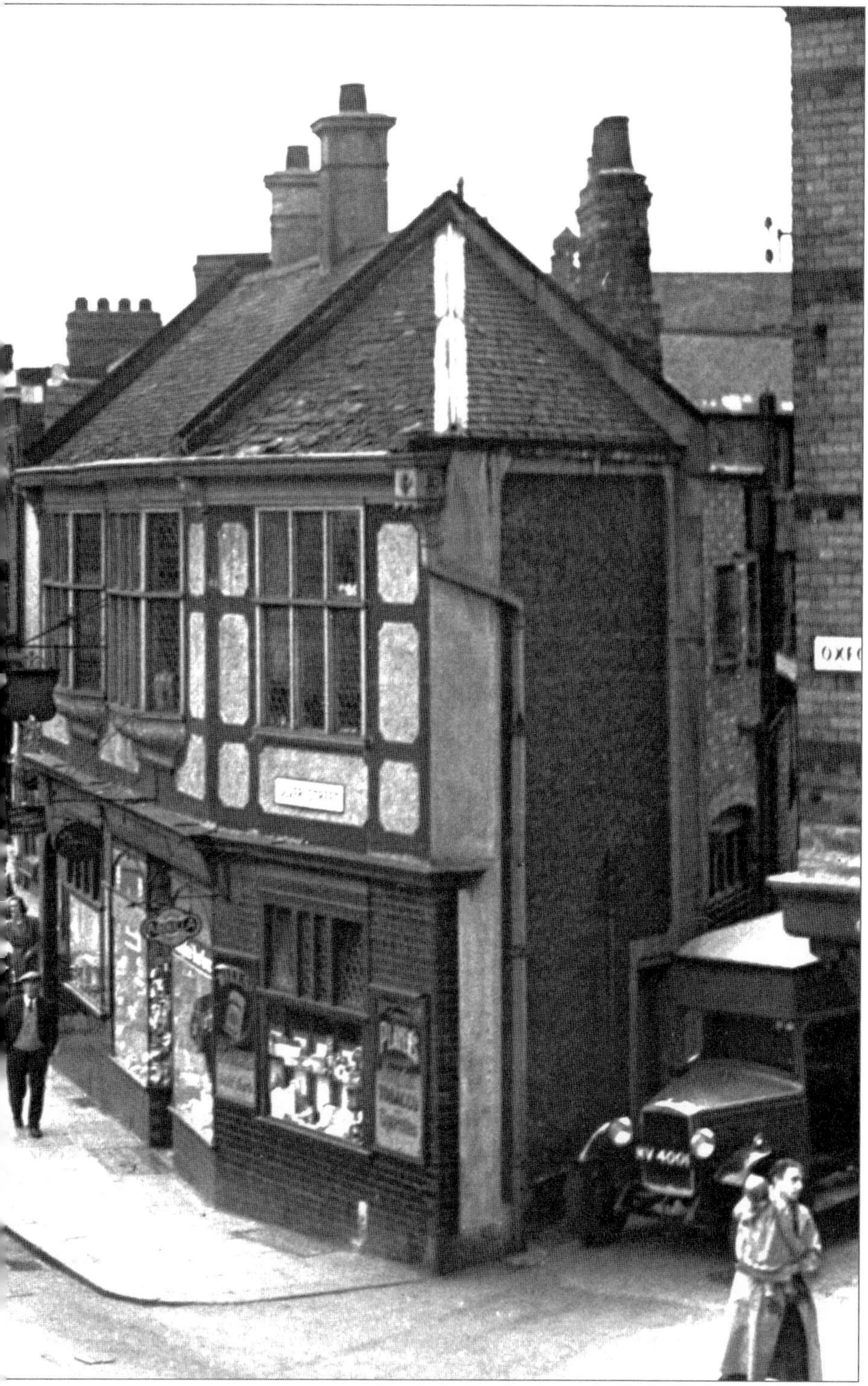

SILVER STREET

c1950 W279005

Further north along Silver Street, at the junction with Oxford Street, Frith's photographer was looking past The Angel Hotel on the left with its rendered front towards Market Street. The Angel was an 18th-century coaching inn, and in later years a receiving office for the London and North Western Railway, with a horse-drawn coach service to the London Road Station. In this view it was in its last years as a hotel: it closed in the late 1950s,and its ground floor was converted to shops, including a Co-op.

▼ **OXFORD STREET** *c1950* W279007

18th- and early 19th-century development along Oxford Street, the main road west from the town, was supplemented and gaps filled by very different more ornate and larger scale Victorian buildings - the four-gabled one (centre left) is dated 1889. One or two large early Victorian mansions survive, such as the one with numerous chimneystacks in the distance, now the Kenroyal Nursing Home. The two-gabled garage building on the left of about 1890 was demolished recently and replaced by a somewhat pedestrian Morrison's supermarket.

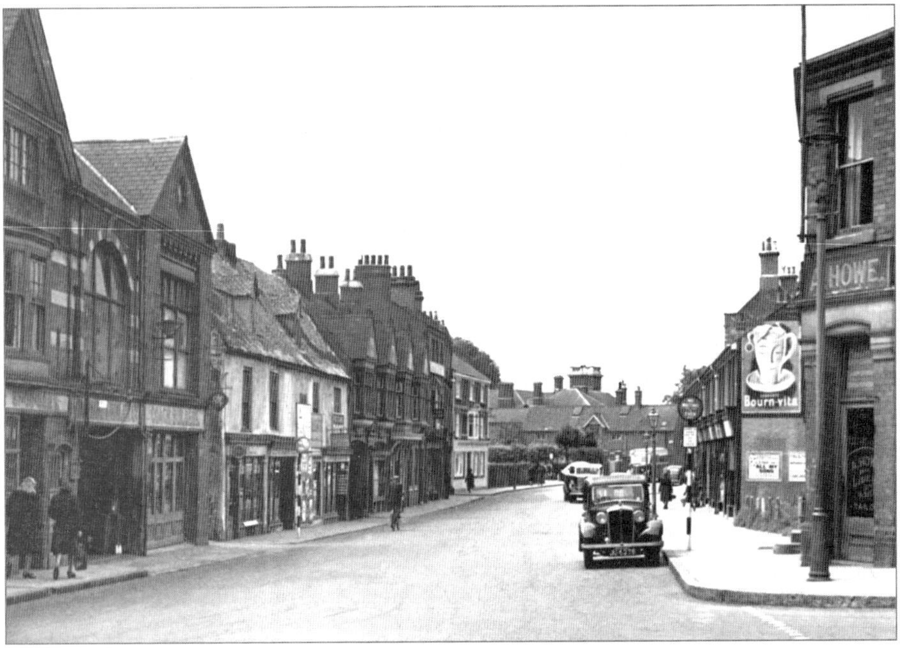

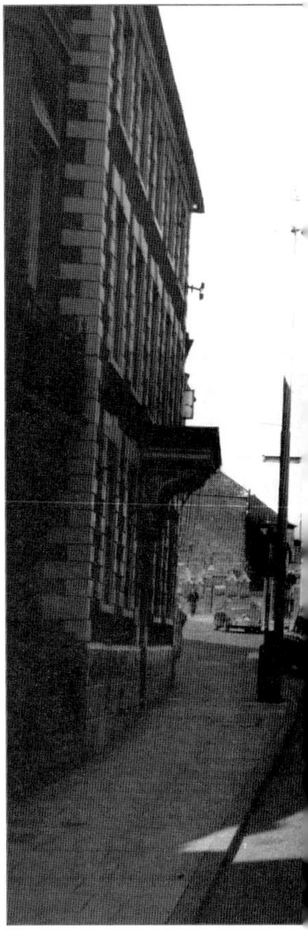

▶ **HIGH STREET**
c1950 W279006

The High Street runs northwards from the Oxford Street/Silver Street junction - it is quite steep at this point. The building with the heavy bracketed balcony and two gabled bay windows (left) is the former Conservative Club of 1882, designed by Talbot Brown, who also designed Wellingborough School (view W279036, page 26). It is now the Royal British Legion Club. On the right is a terrace of 1883 in typical hard red Midland brick; there is now only one original shopfront still intact, the third one from the right.

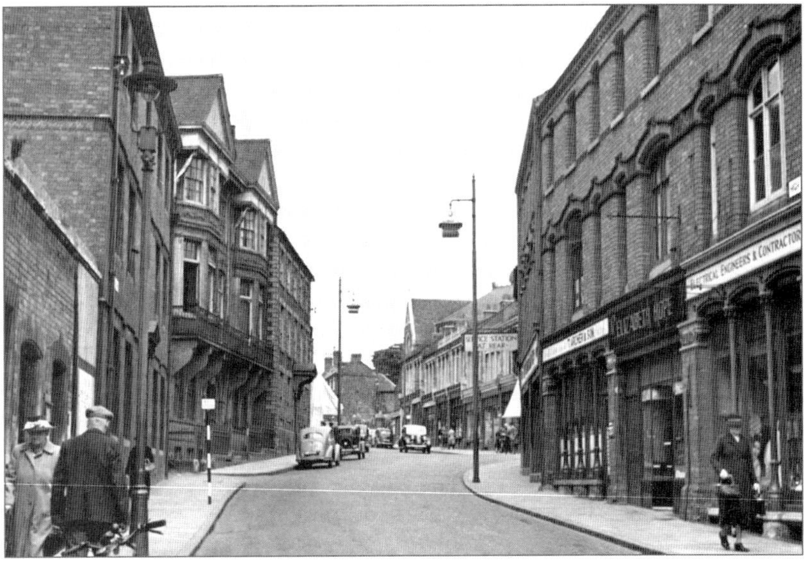

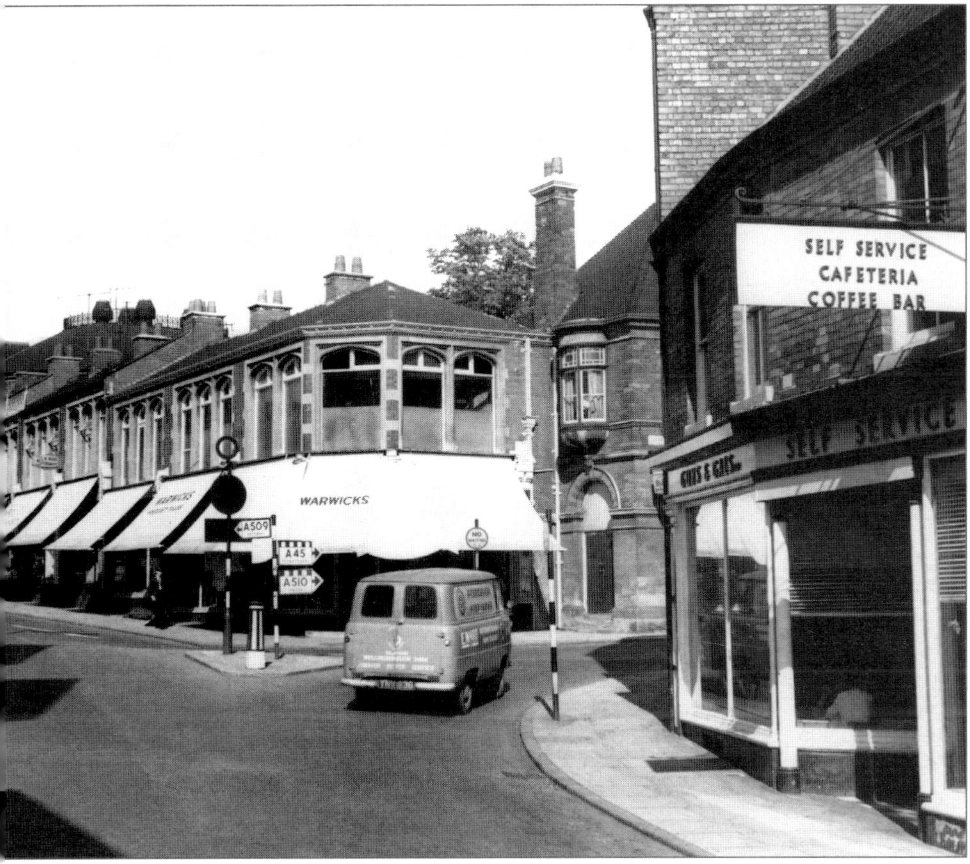

◄ HIGH STREET
c1965 W279062

We are a little further uphill than view W279006 (page 36). The Bedford van is turning right into Church Street with the early 1880s Warwicks shop on the corner, part of a Venetian Gothic-influenced terrace that steps up the hill. The Congregational church gable rises beyond. Warwicks was a tailor, hatter and hosier, but is still in business today as a dress-hire shop - the shop blinds have been replaced by a deep blue fascia. On the left is a fine late 18th-century town house, Leighton House.

► THE CONGREGATIONAL CHURCH
c1955 W279045

Past Warwicks dress-hire shop we reach the Congregational church, with Queen Street to its right and Salem Lane to the left. This is now the United Reformed church - the Congregationals merged with the Presbyterians in the mid 20th century. It has an unusual plan, an egg-shaped nave with gabled staircase wings or transepts attached, all in Gothic style. Built in local yellowish ironstone and white limestone dressings, it dates from 1875.

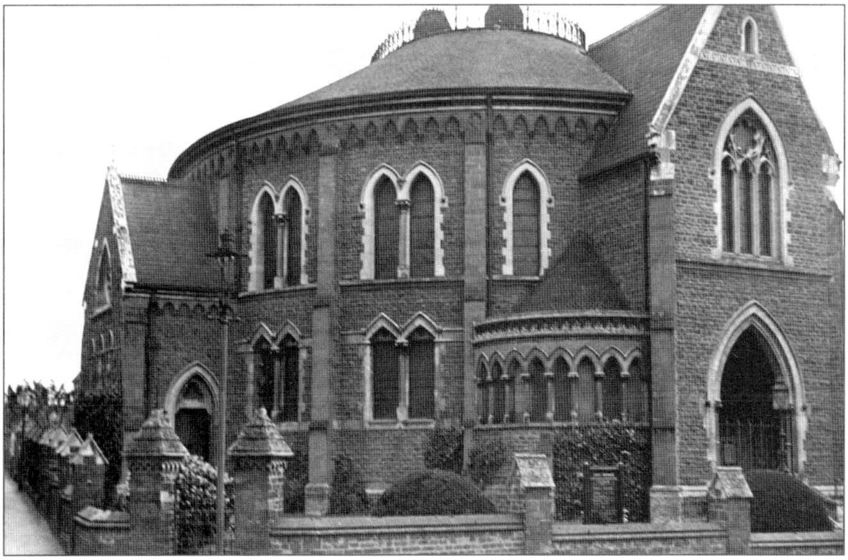

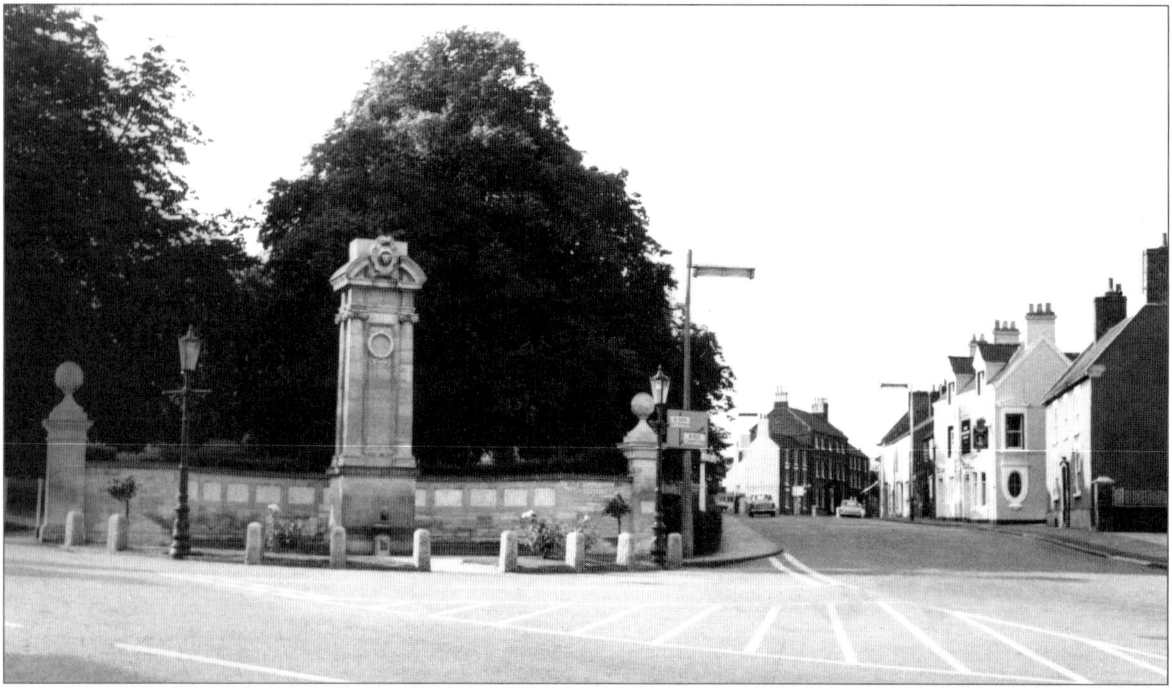

▲ **BROAD GREEN**
The War Memorial c1965 W279110

The High Street climbs gently to Broad Green, passing along a street with some of the best 18th- and 19th-century houses in the town, to end in a well-treed triangular green where the road forks. Good ironstone houses continue along Hatton Gardens, on the right, while the south corner of the green is now occupied by the war memorial, installed in 1924. The fine trees remain. On the north side of the green is Hatton Hall, of which only the 19th-century stone Tudor-style facade survived conversion into flats in the early 1980s.

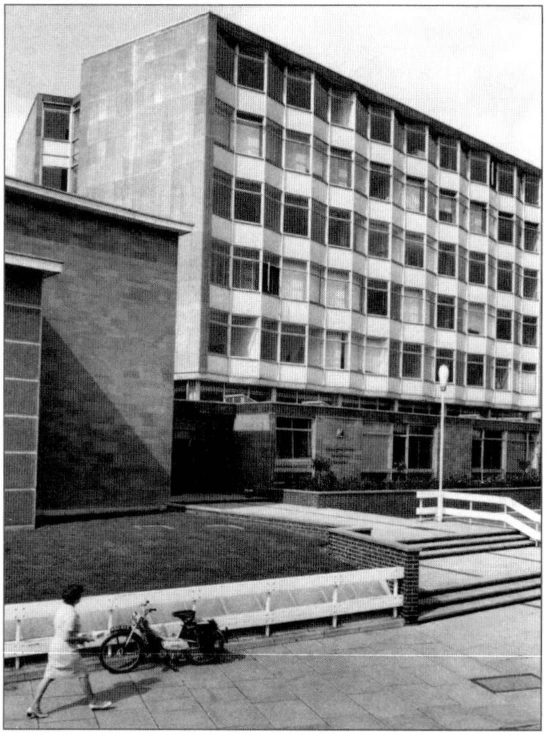

► **THE TECHNICAL COLLEGE**
c1965 W279121

Back towards the town centre, we turn into Church Street; here, on the north side, the new Wellingborough was arriving in the mid 1960s. The old Technical Institute, a dour Midland brick Victorian building, was demolished once the new Technical College was completed behind it. The left-hand building was first, in 1961, and the six storey block to the right was completed in 1964, both designed by the County Architect; the buildings are now the Tresham Institute, Wellingborough Campus. The roof of the tall block now sports numerous satellite and mobile phone antennae to give it a more spiky roofline.

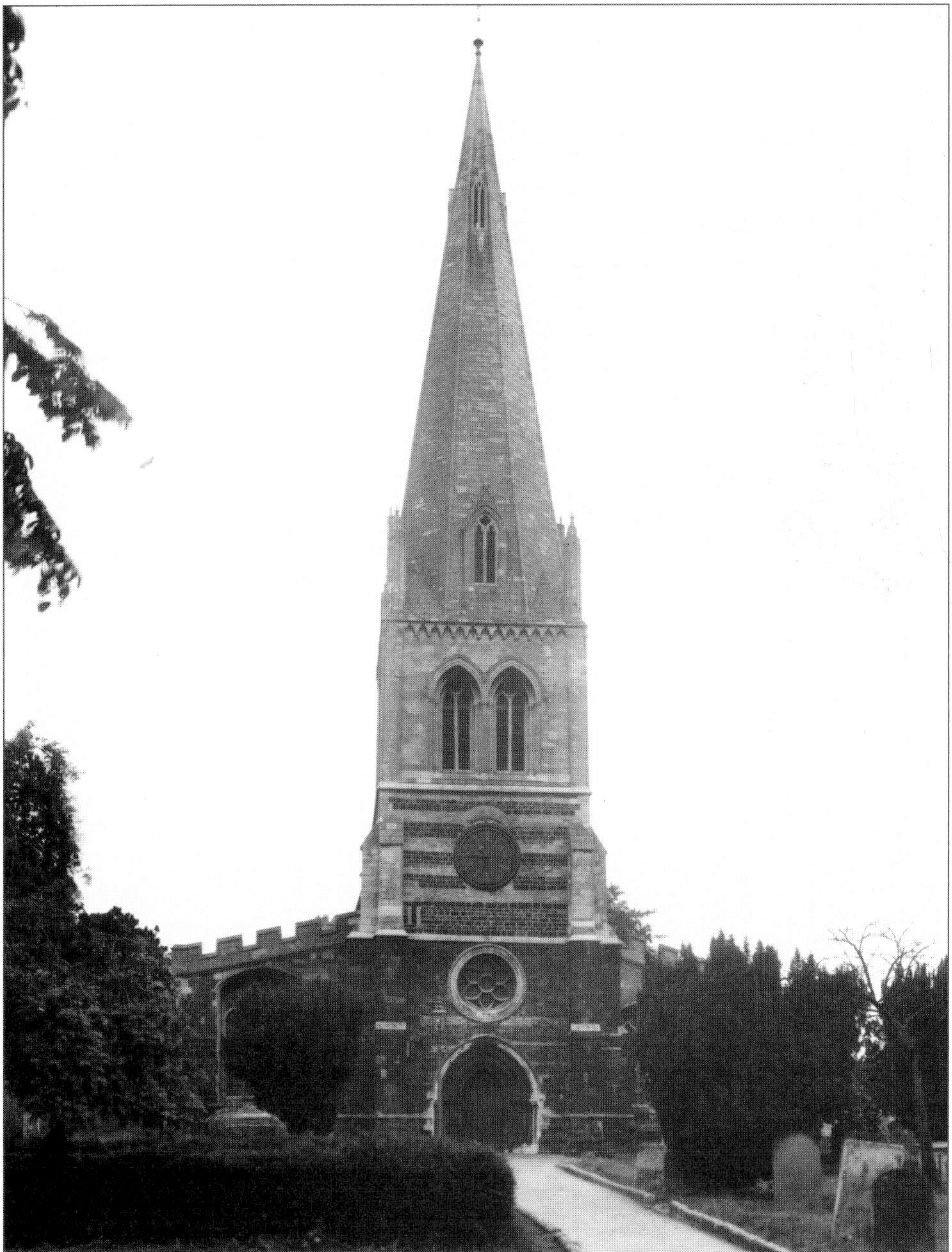

ALL HALLOWS PARISH CHURCH *c1955* W279042

Between Church Street and the market place is the green haven of All Hallows churchyard. To its north-west stands the old grammar school, a typical Northamptonshire 17th-century banded ironstone building of 1620. The church retains a Norman doorway, but is mostly late 13th-century with a fine spire, all in white limestone. The clock face below the belfry windows is in local cast iron and is dated 1871.

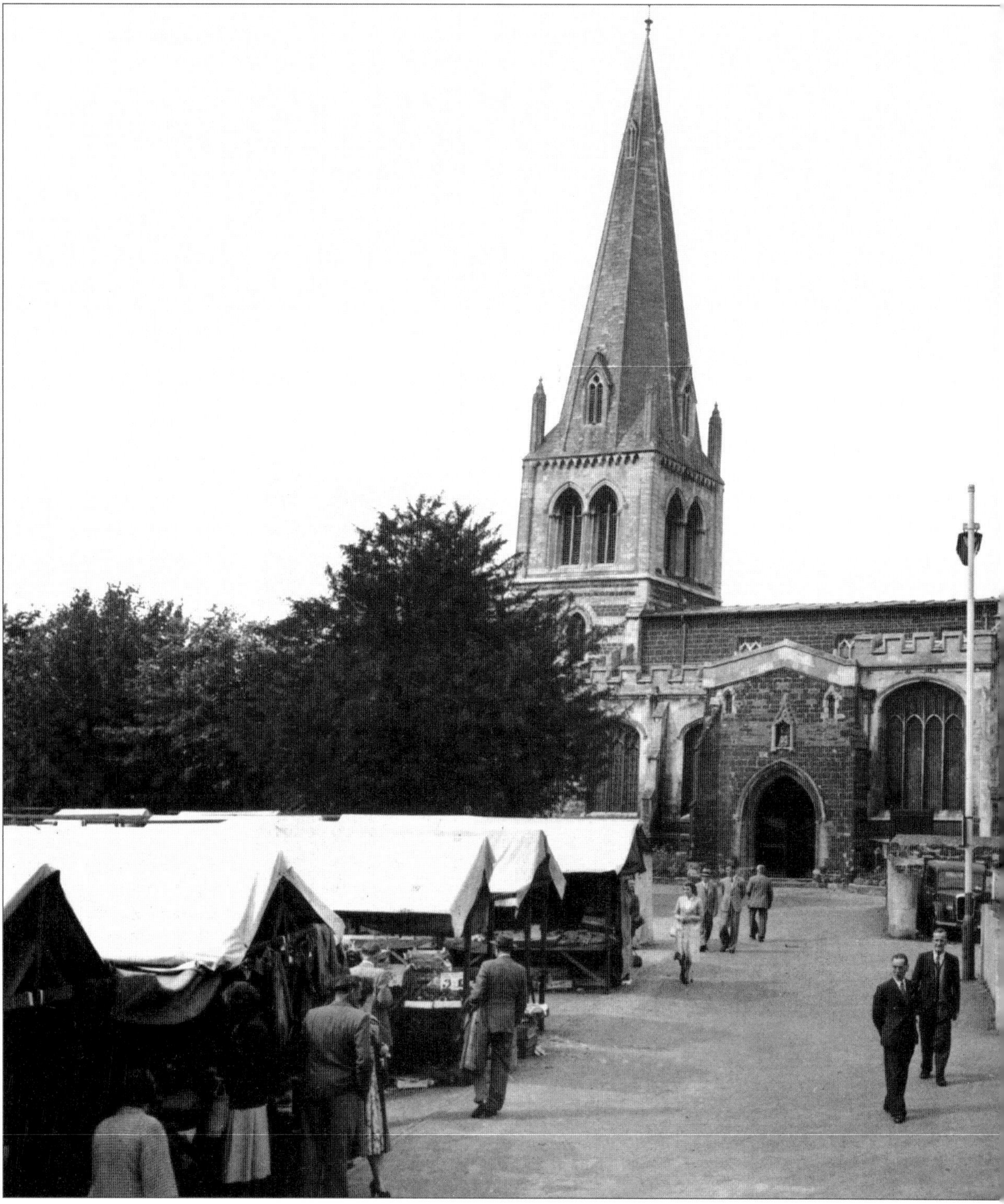

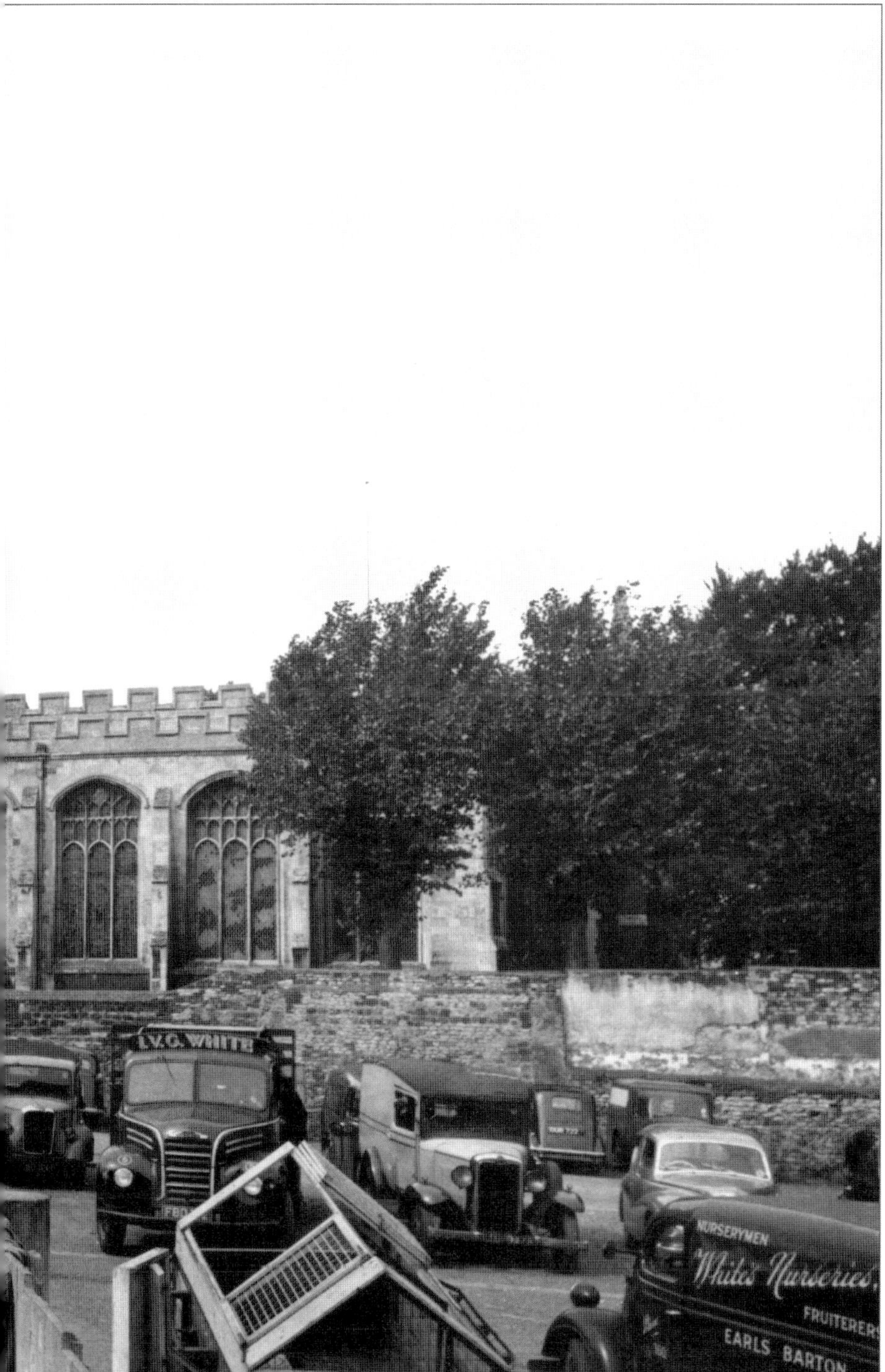

ALL HALLOWS PARISH CHURCH FROM THE MARKET PLACE

c1955 W279051

The market place is south of the churchyard. The churchyard wall has been rebuilt with iron railings and stone gate piers since the mid 1970s. This area is still the market place: stalls are set up on Wednesdays, Fridays and Saturdays, with a bric-a-brac market on Tuesdays.

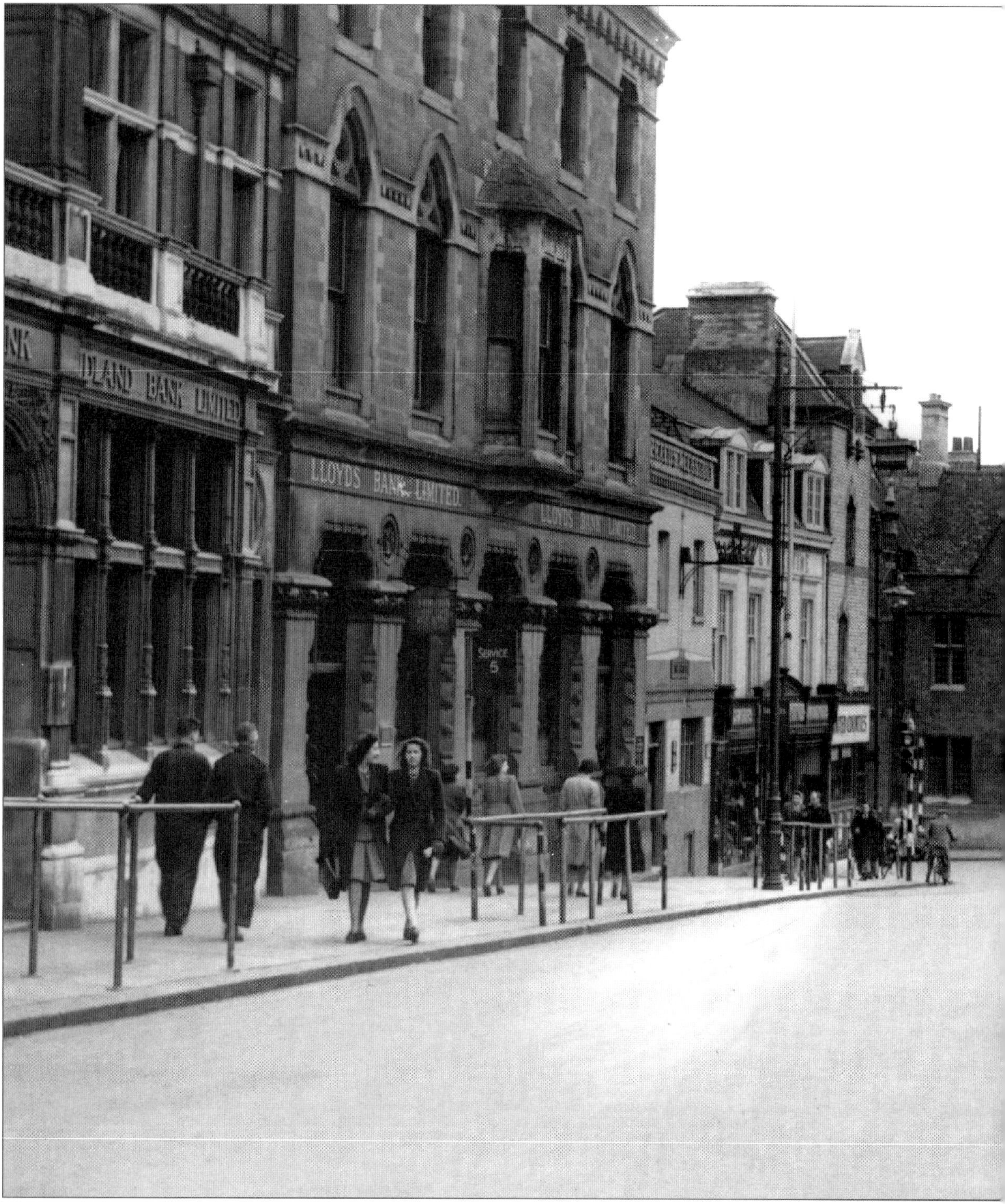
DLAND BANK LIMITED
LLOYDS BANK LIMITED.
LLOYDS BANK LIMITED
SERVICE
5

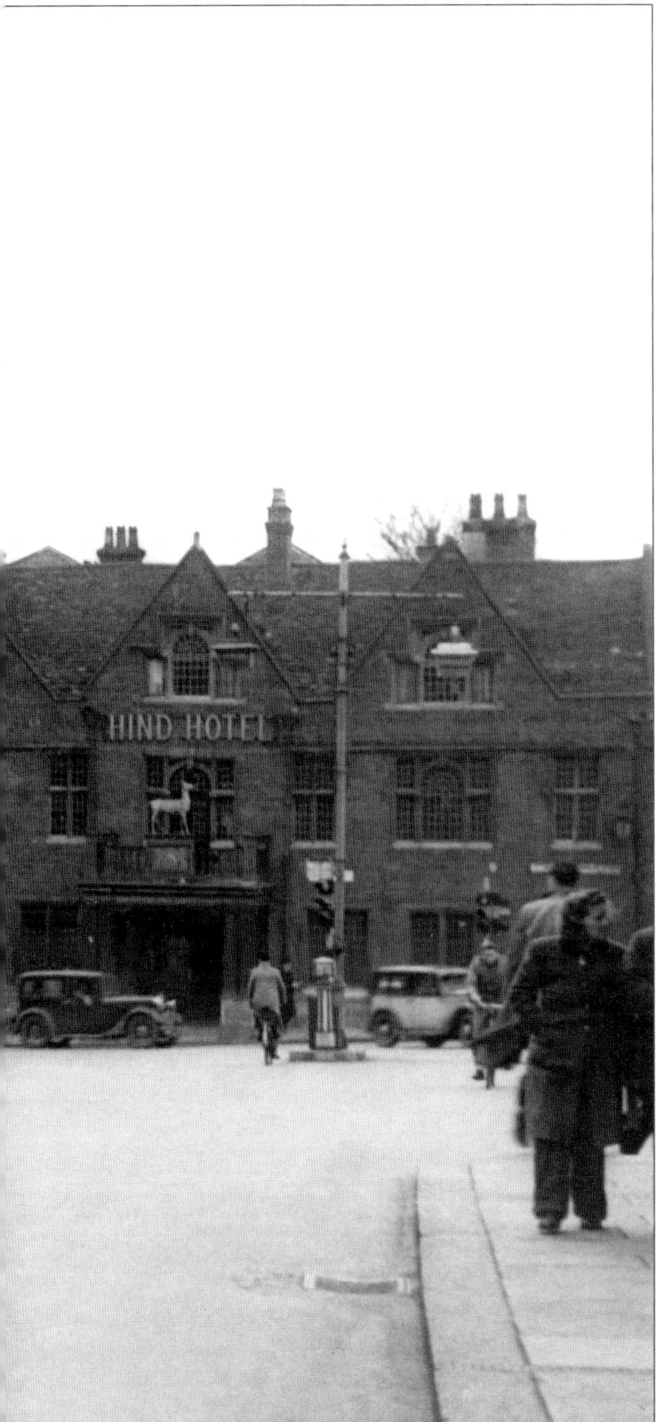

EASTWARDS FROM MARKET STREET

MARKET STREET *c1950* W279004

The third chapter starts at the south-west end of Market Street. This was where the medieval market place was located - the present market place is just a northward arm from it. The old medieval market cross stood roughly where the traffic island is (centre right), but it was demolished in 1798 as a traffic hazard. The market had been established by a charter granted by King John in 1201, so it has had a long history; there was initially only a weekly market on a Wednesday.

MARKET STREET
c1955 W279049

This view from Sheep Street looks north across the market square. The clock tower of the Corn Exchange peers over the corrugated roof of one of the buildings severely damaged and truncated by the 1942 bomb which fell on the market place. The Corn Exchange, built in 1861 and later adapted into the Regal Cinema, survived the war but was demolished in 1959. It was replaced by a very dull supermarket, which was demolished in its turn in 1995.

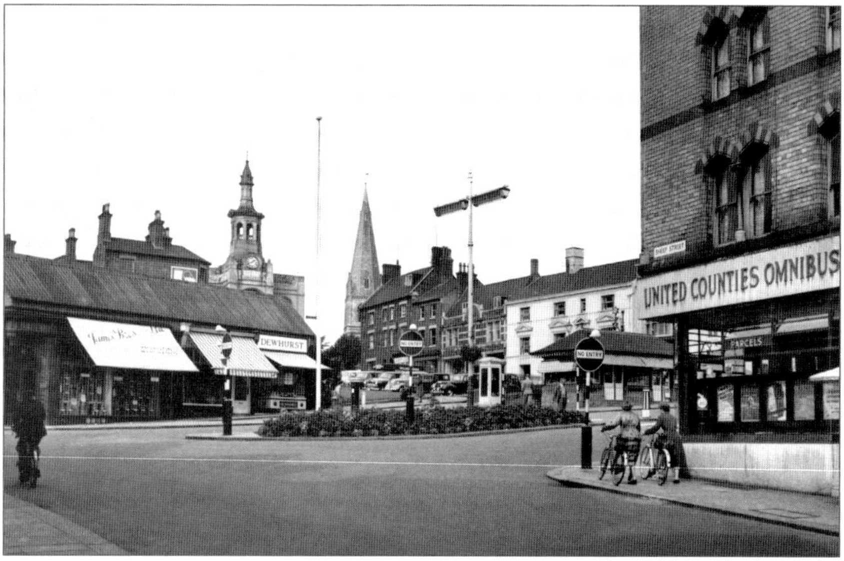

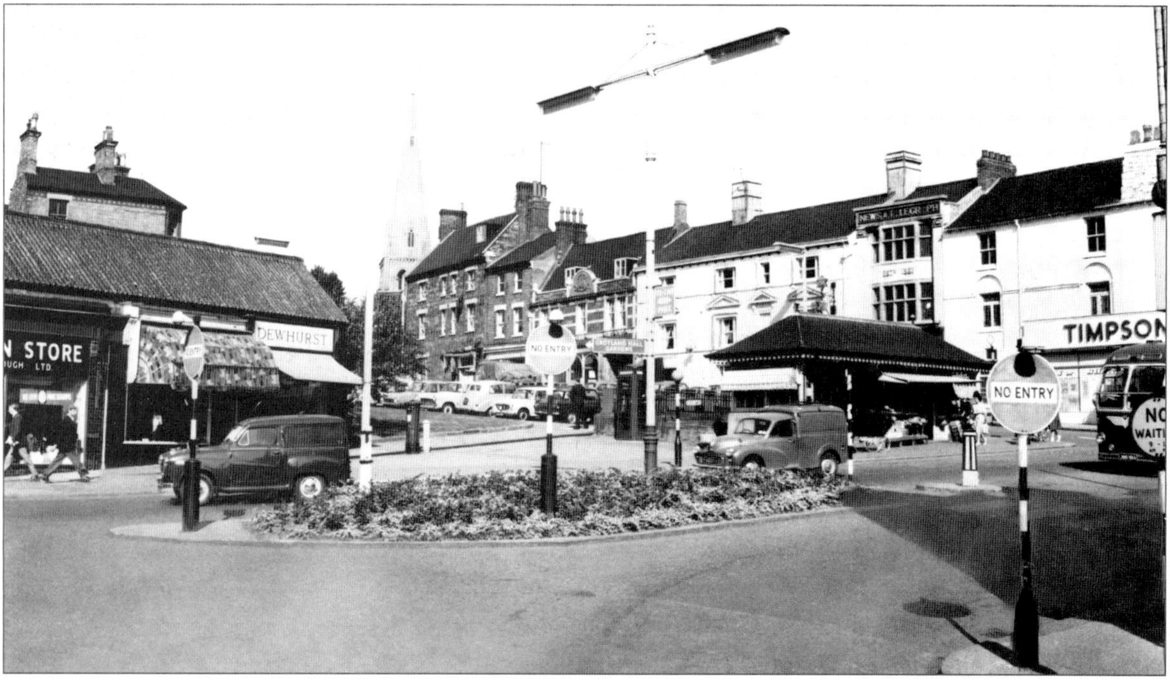

MARKET STREET *c1965* W279060

Only the parish church and the Pagoda survive of the buildings shown in this mid 1960s view. The Pagoda is the small building with the hipped roof (behind the Morris van, centre right); it was built as a bus shelter, but by the 1950s it had become a newsagent's shop. The buildings on the left were demolished to make way for a MacDonalds. The ones on the right, which included several old buildings and the white stuccoed Exchange Hotel, went in 1974 to be replaced by the present dull Woolworth's and Barclays Bank block.

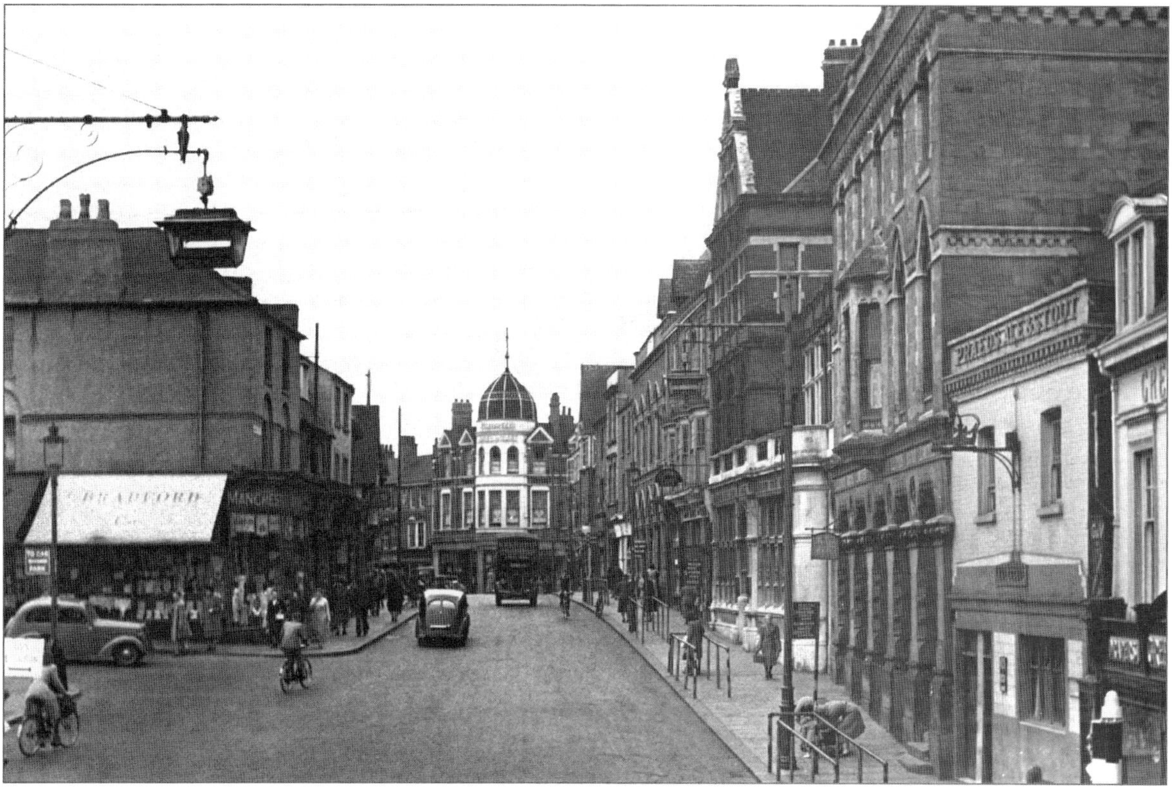

MARKET STREET *c1955* W279031

Now Frith's photographer was looking towards the impressive corner tower of the Granville at the junction with Midland Road. The market square and Market Street as far as Midland Road have now been pedestrianised, but this is poor recompense for the wholesale destruction of the heart of the town. In the 1970s all between Midland Road and the tall gabled building on the right was demolished for the Swansgate Shopping Centre, and the three buildings in the left foreground were replaced by the Woolworth's and Barclays Bank block. This was quite apart from the depredations in the market place itself.

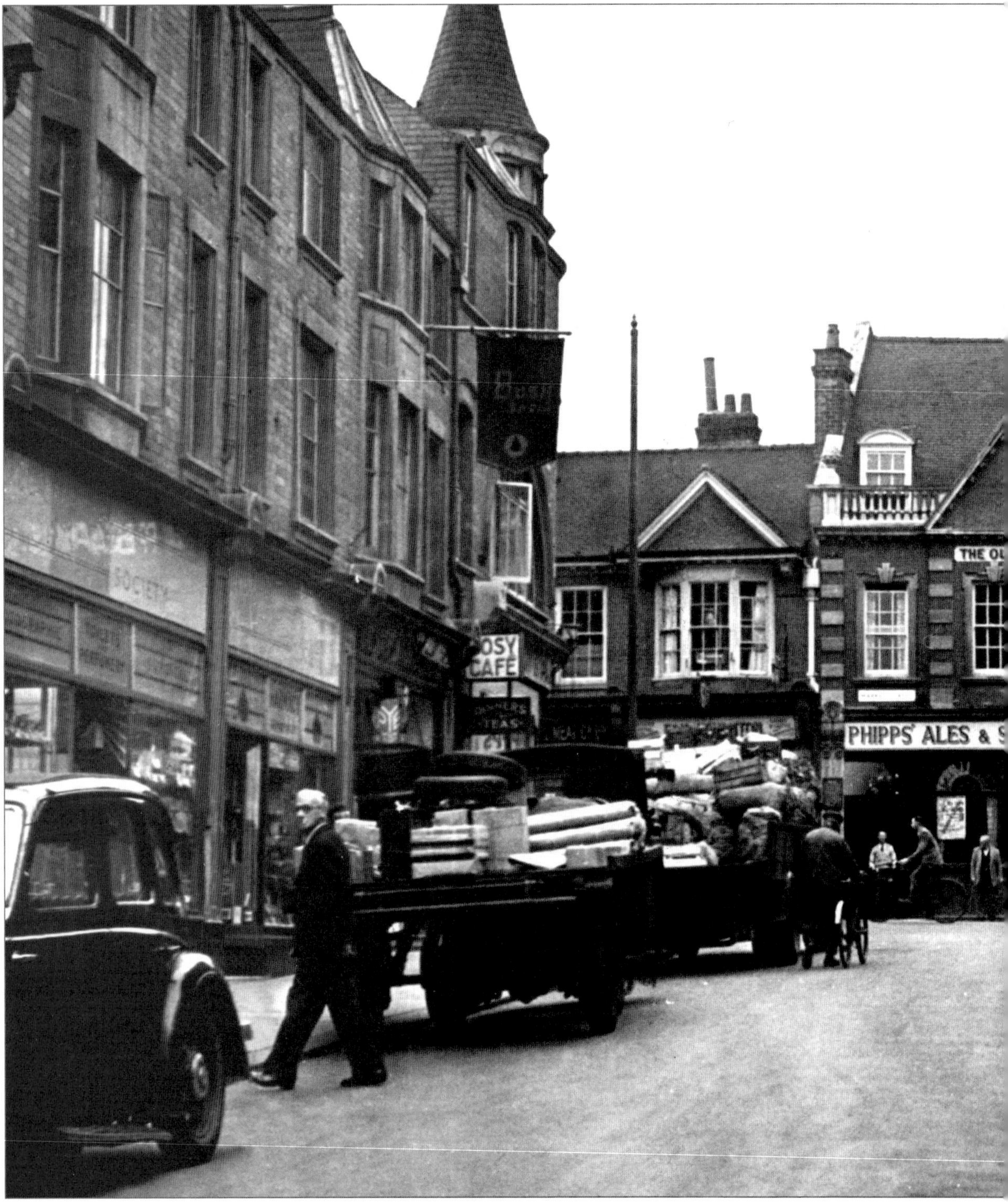
OSY
CAFE
PHIPPS' ALES &
THE OL

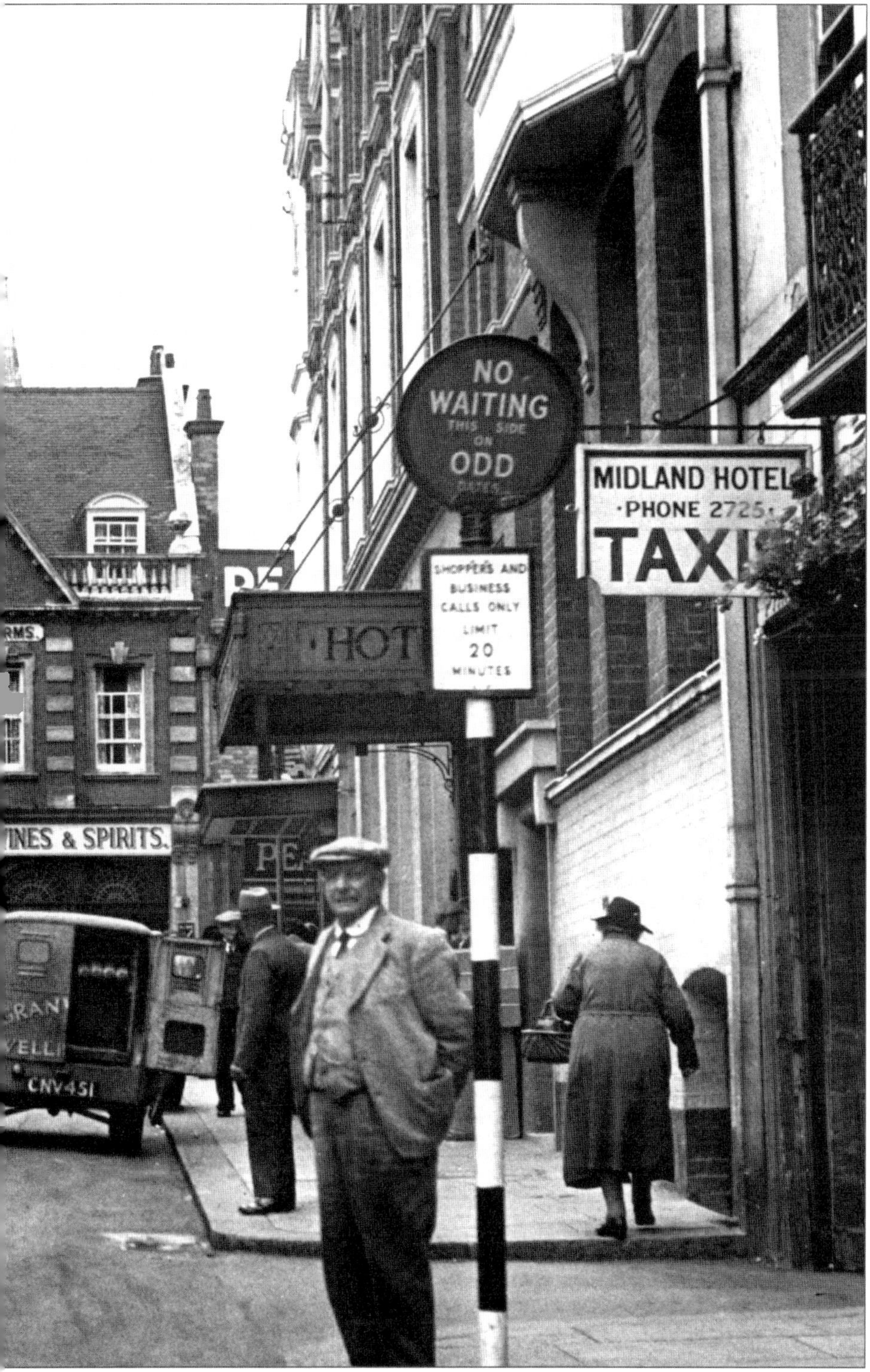

MIDLAND ROAD
c1950 W279025

Midland Road was formed in the early 1860s after the Midland Railway station opened half a mile east of the town centre. It grew rapidly, with the end nearer Market Street becoming one of the town's busiest shopping streets. You would not know it nowadays, for the Swansgate Shopping Centre resulted in all the buildings on the left side of the road being replaced by the shopping mall's largely blank side elevation.

MIDLAND ROAD *c1955*
W279046

On the right side of the road, the Post Office dates from 1908. The stuccoed 1860s Midland Hotel to its left is now demolished and replaced by a 1960s post office of a mean two storeys set back from the road frontage. All on the left went in 1974 for the Swansgate Centre, of course, but The Old King's Arms pub in Market Street closing the vista up Midland Road survives. Built in Queen Anne style around 1890, it was converted by the 1970s to shops, currently empty (October 2003).

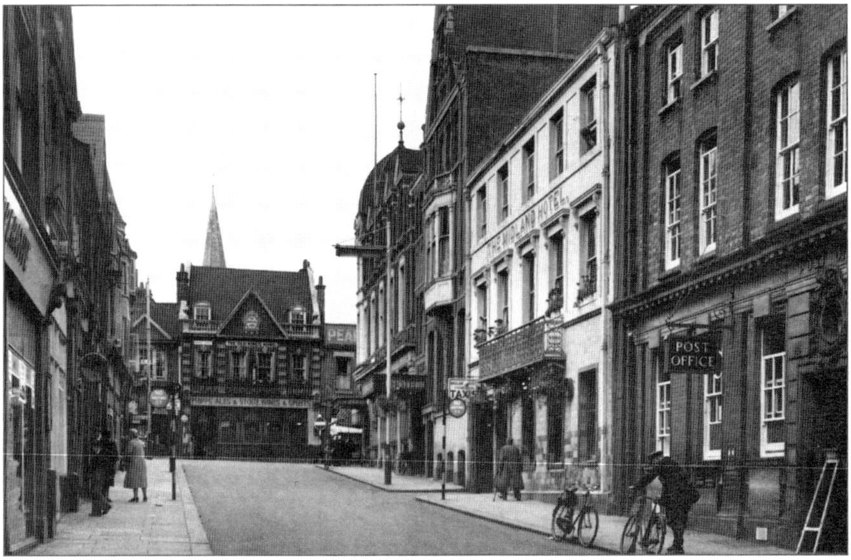

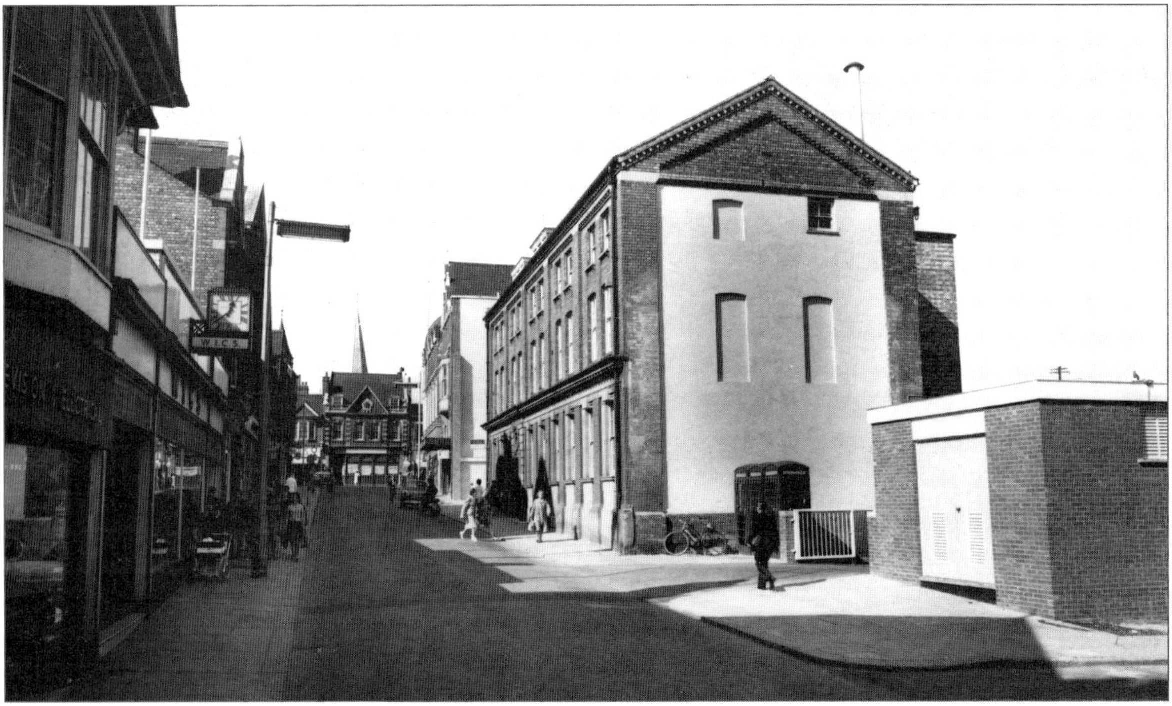

MIDLAND ROAD *c1965* W279068

Everything on the left side of the road was demolished in 1974 to make way for the Arndale Centre's shopping malls, later renamed the Swansgate Shopping Centre, an inward-looking building that does nothing for the vibrancy of the streets around it. On the right is the tall brick former Post Office. The area in front was shortly to be filled by the dominating five-storey Telephone Exchange block, which was completed in 1971.

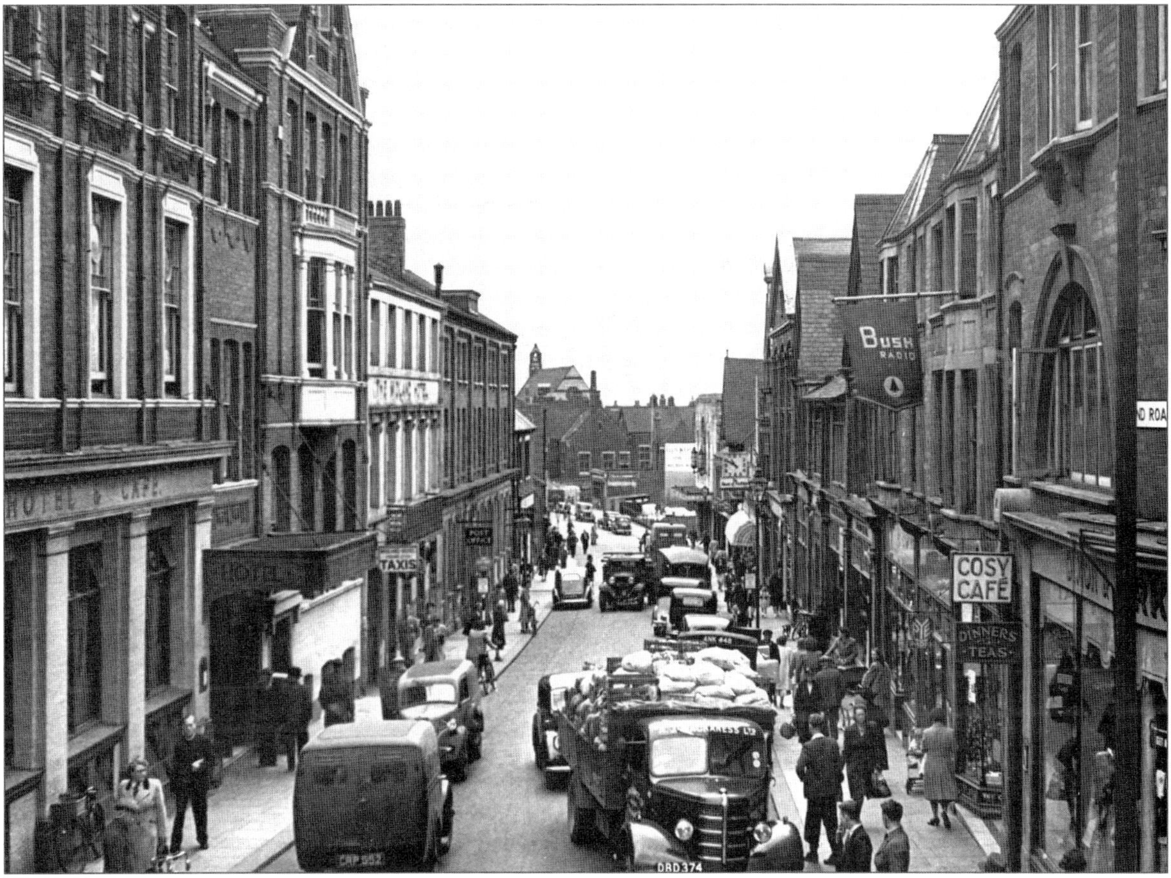

MIDLAND ROAD *c1950* W279024

Walking down Midland Road from the Market Street end today, it is difficult to envisage it as one of the busiest shopping streets in the town as it was in this 1950s view. All on the right was replaced by the blank Swansgate Shopping Centre exterior which opened in 1977, and the middle distance is a gap filled by Commercial Way which cuts through to Sheep Street. Beyond is the bellcote of All Saints parish church, built in the 1860s to serve the Victorian eastern expansion of the town towards the railway.

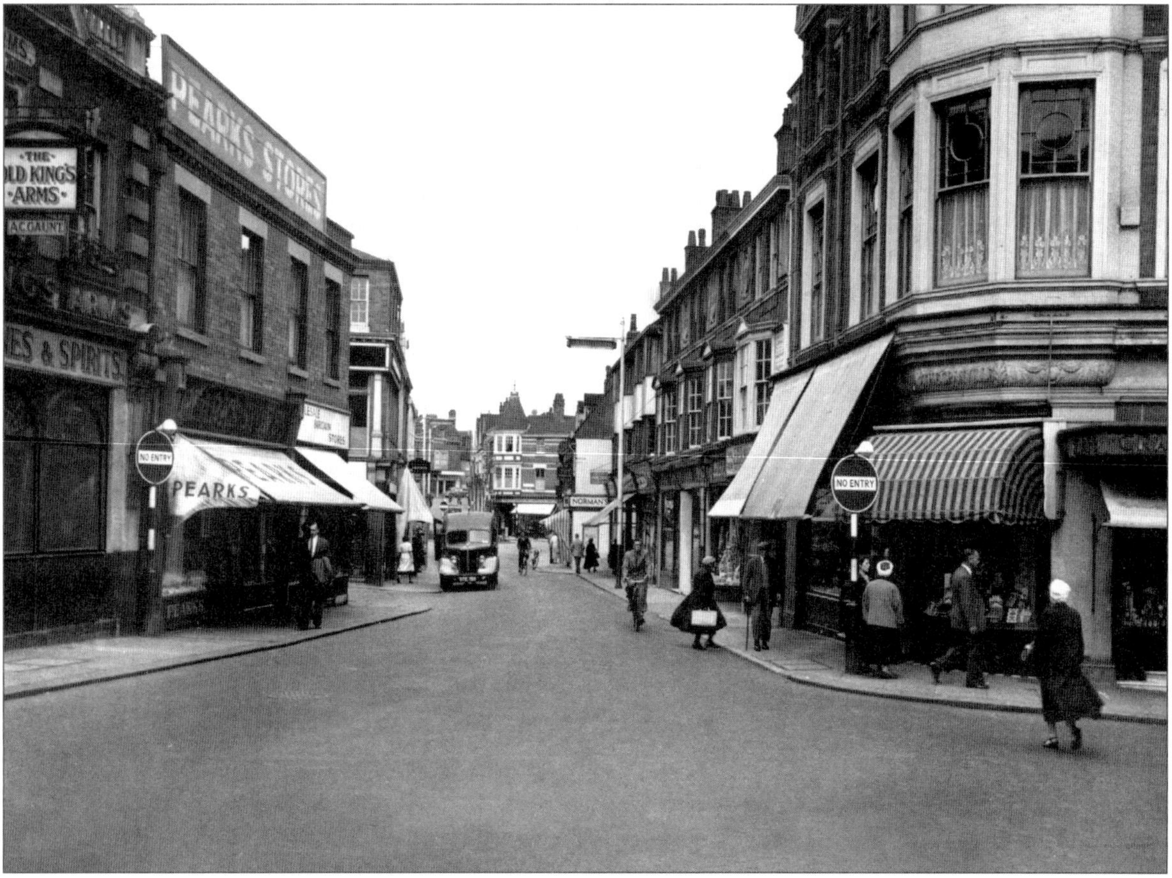

MARKET STREET *c1955* W279047

This view looks towards Gloucester Place in the distance from the corner of Midland Road, with The Old King's Arms on the left and Pearks Stores beyond, now a Shoefayre with a modern shopfront. On the right is the lower part of the ornate corner oriel that finishes in the dome seen in view W279031 (page 39). This was part of The Granville, which had been built in 1882 as a temperance hotel and cafe, with shops on the ground floor. It is now a Burton's menswear shop, and a modern fascia hides the ornate lower part of the oriel.

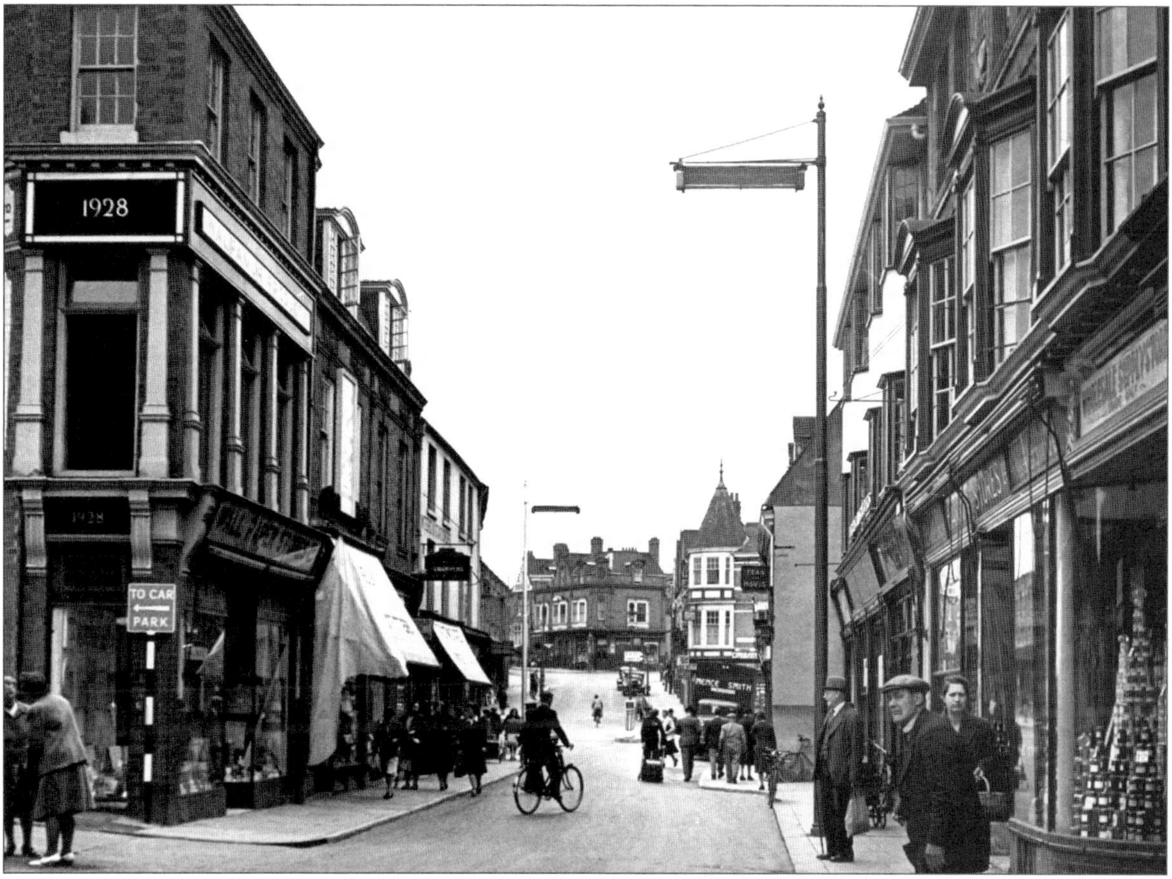

MARKET STREET *c1955* W279027

The fine shopfronts on the right belong to the former Ceylon House, which was built in 1901 on the site of The White Horse Inn. The bay windows and everything above survive today, but the shopfronts have been altered. The Wall Paper Stores (left) with its two-storeyed shopfront is clearly dated 1928, although all this is now painted over and is now an optician's. The roadway has recently been re-laid with brick paviours and is now one-way, curving into Midland Road.

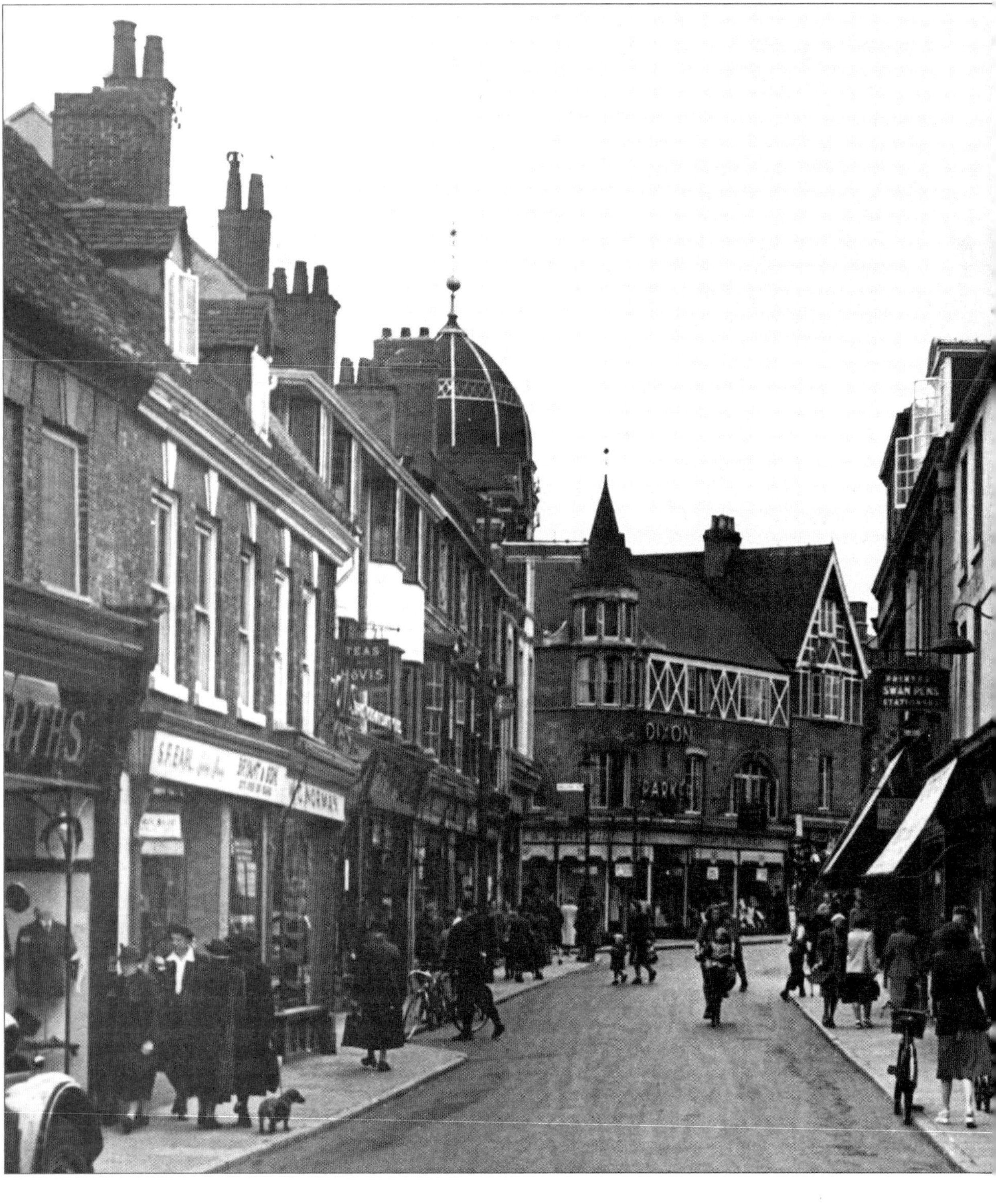
S.F. EARL
TEAS
HOVIS
DIXON
PARKS
SWAN PENS

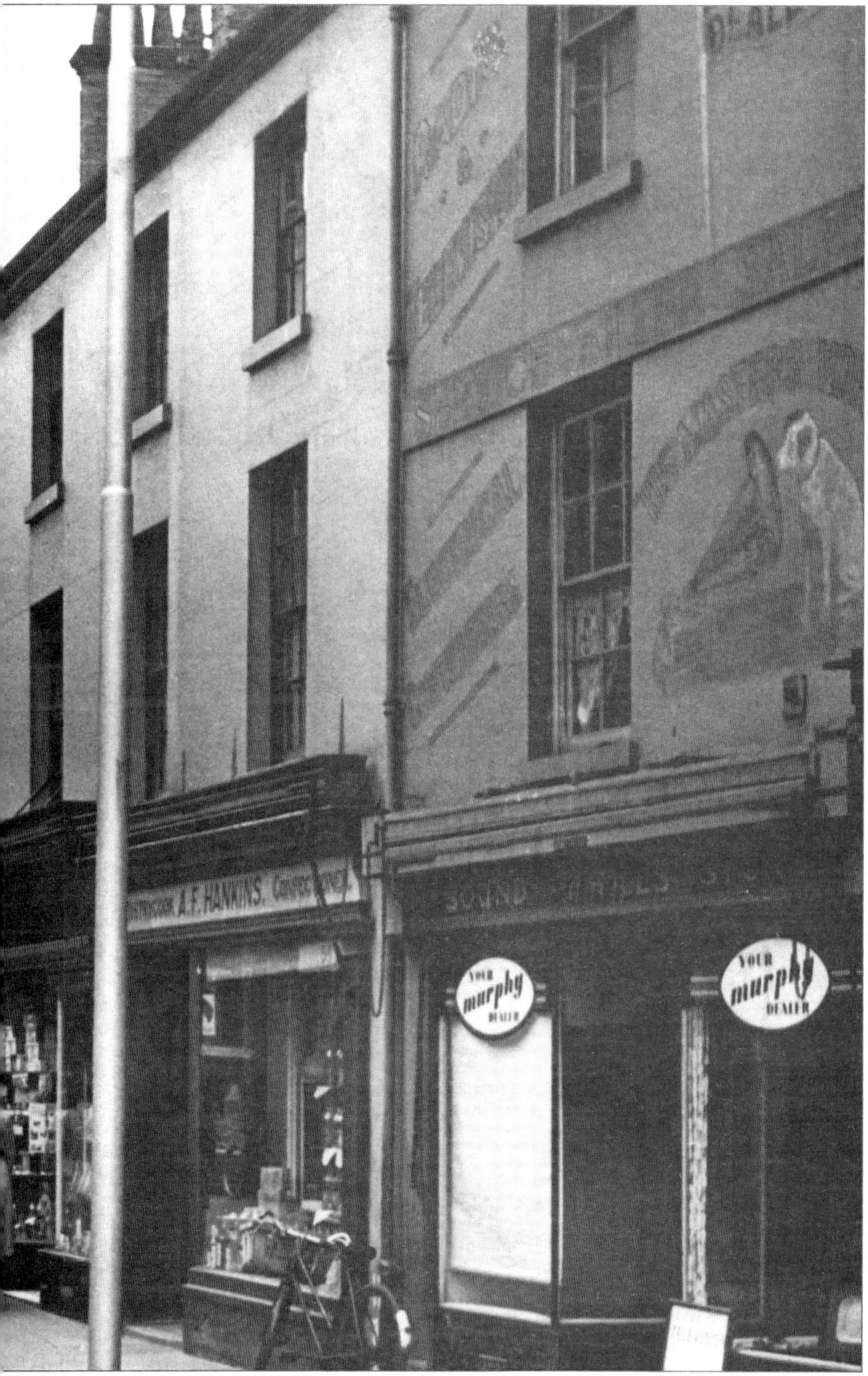

MARKET STREET

c1955 W279029

Now at the Gloucester Place end of Market Street, Frith's photographer was looking past the 18th- and 19th-century houses with a variety of later shopfronts to the building on the corner of Midland Road with the corner turret and timber-framing. This was Dixon and Parker's men's outfitter's; it was built about 1890, but along with everything else nearby on this corner, it was demolished in 1974 for the Arndale Centre which opened in 1977, now the Swansgate Shopping Centre. The loss of all these buildings at the heart of the town did severe damage to its historic character.

▶ **GLOUCESTER PLACE** *c1965* W279065

Market Street reaches Gloucester Place, an area formed by the junction with Cambridge and Church Streets, and continues north as Alma Street, presumably named after the Crimean War battle of Alma which took place in 1854. This view from Market Street looks across to the Palace, which opened in 1911 and was later converted to a cinema. At the time of the photograph it was showing the horror film *The Two Faces of Dr Jekyll.* Nowadays (2003) it is the Palace Snooker and Pool Centre, its grand entrance bay mutilated (or modernised).

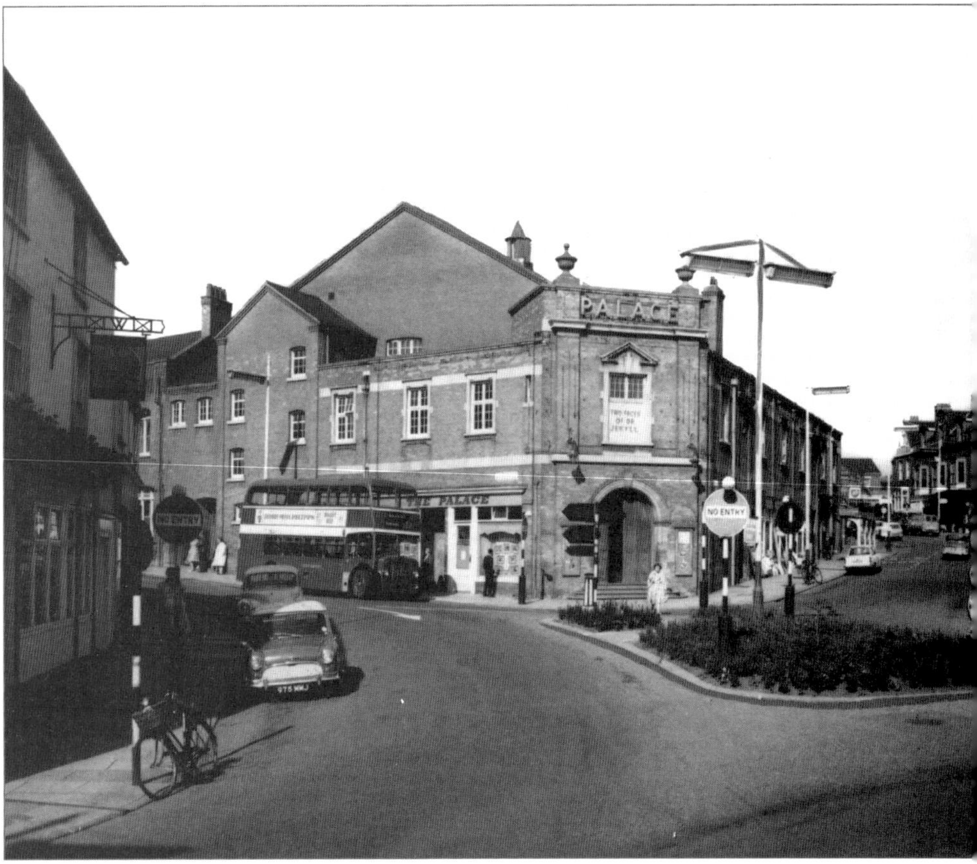

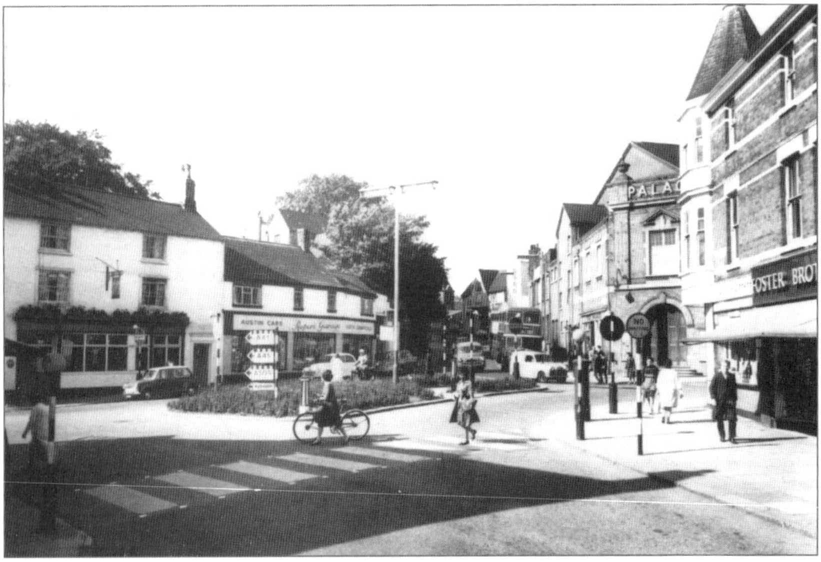

◀ **GLOUCESTER PLACE** *c1965* W279066

This second view in Gloucester Place looks from Cambridge Street across into Church Street, with The Globe pub, an early 19th-century building, on the left. Beyond the Palace cinema (right) is the Gloucester Club of 1882 and its Hall which was added in 1925; The Fiddlers Elbow pub is in the far distance. The turret on the right is at the corner of a terrace of about 1880. Dudeney & Johnson below it and Foster Brothers menswear next door have gone, being replaced by a sports shop and a computer shop respectively.

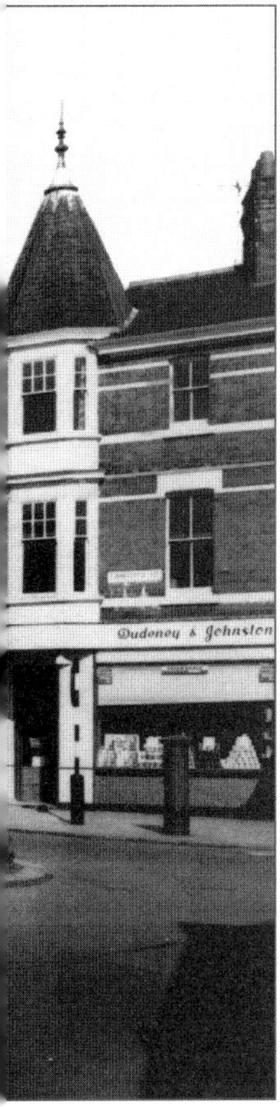

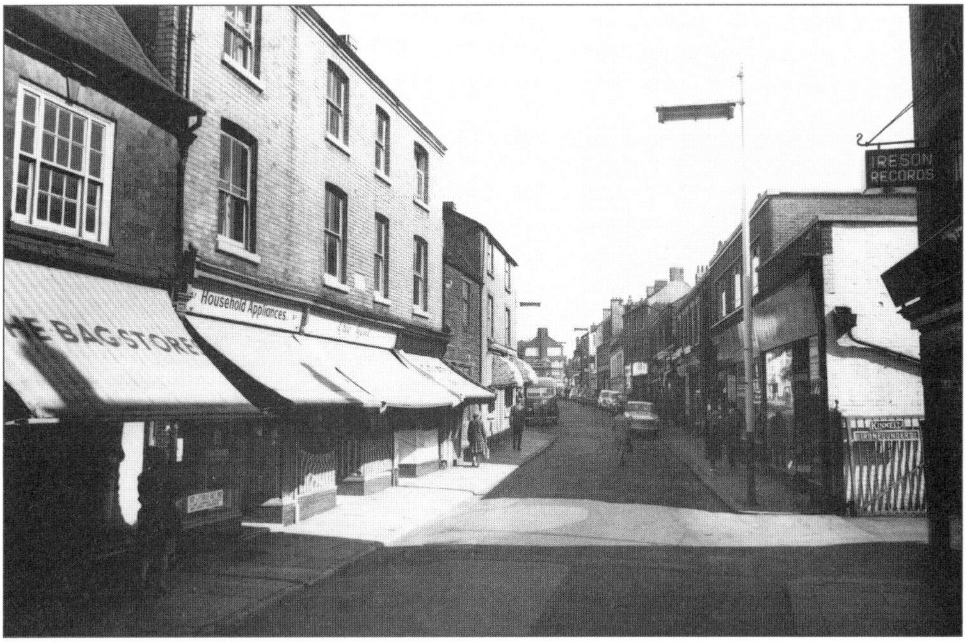

▲ **CAMBRIDGE STREET** *c1965* W279067

Cambridge Street runs east from Gloucester Place, and was once the main road to Irthlingborough, but it is now merely a bridleway east of the railway until it merges with the present less direct route, the B571. The street is lined with many 18th- and 19th-century former houses, including the late 18th-century ironstone one, The Bagstore (now The Studio) at the far left with its distinctive tripartite sash window. The road is now surfaced in brick paviours. At the far end is the gable of The Rising Sun pub.

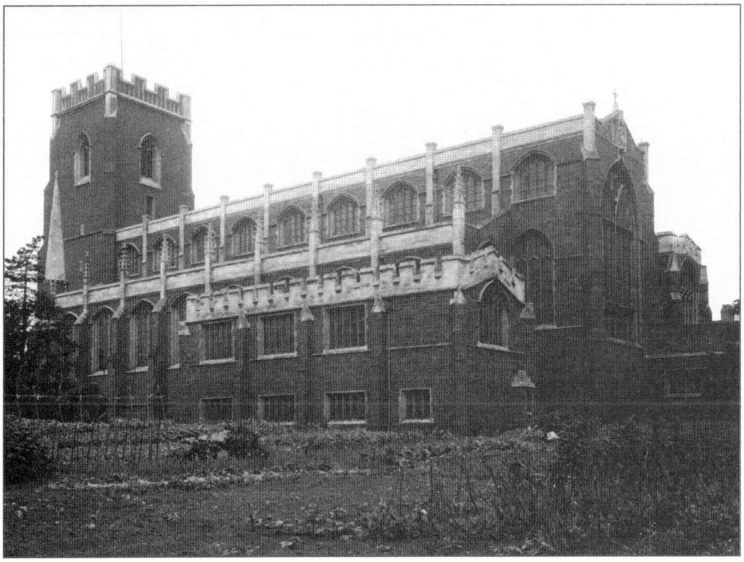

◀ **ST MARY'S CHURCH**
c1955 W279034

As Wellingborough expanded eastwards, St Mary's parish was created; its church was built at the junction of Knox Road and Elsdon Road. The whole church was funded by the three Sharman sisters of Elsdon Lodge. Work proceeded slowly to the designs of one of England's most influential church architects, Sir Ninian Comper. The first part to be completed, the chapel dedicated in 1908, is at the right in this view. The tower was completed in 1932, but the superb interior was not completed until the 1960s. A churchyard has now (2003) replaced the allotments, and was laid out when flats were built to the west, roughly in the area where Comper had plans for a religious college.

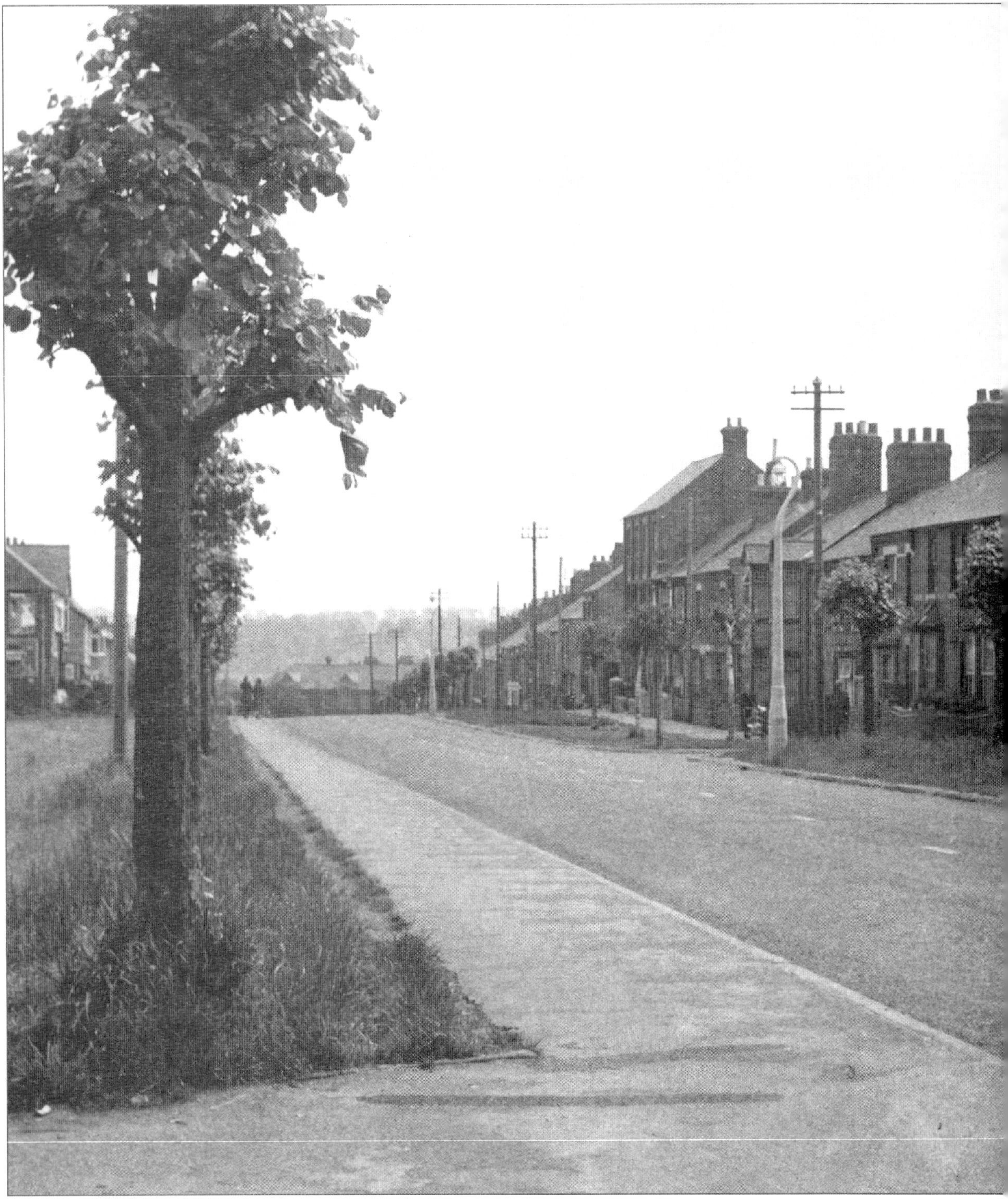

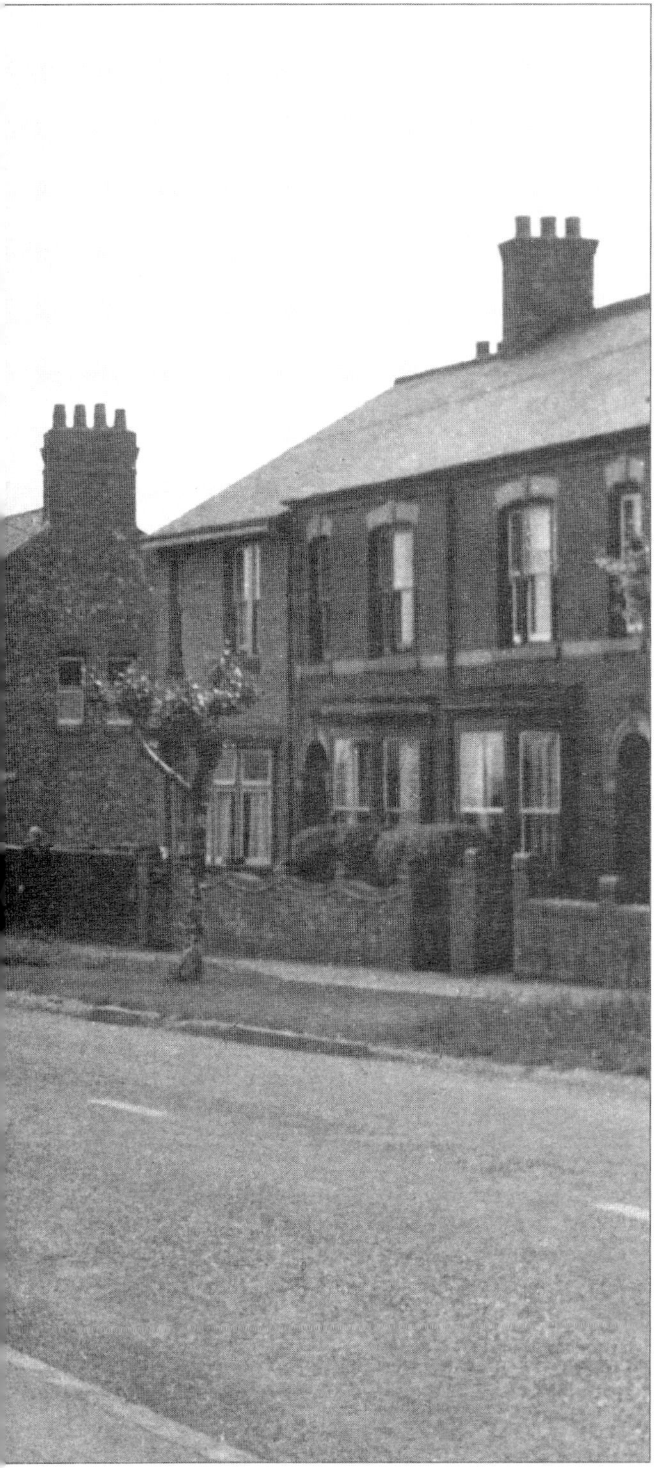

THE NENE VALLEY EAST OF WELLINGBOROUGH

IRCHESTER
Wollaston Road c1955 I71003

The final two chapters in this book leave Wellingborough for two tours along the Nene valley. The first stop is Irchester, a boot and shoe town about three miles to the south-east. The taller building on the right amid the late 19th-century terraces and semis was a shoe factory, but it is now a martial arts centre. On the left is the recreation ground, and in the far distance is the Co-op, dated 1914. This streetscape is typical of the industrial villages of the boot and shoe country: hard red brick houses in grids of streets grafted onto old stone villages.

IRCHESTER
The War Memorial and the Post Office c1960 I71023

Further east, Frith's photographer had turned into the Farndish Road from the Wollaston Road on the left with the post office on the opposite corner (still a post office), and was looking past the 1920s war memorial in its sloping garden with steep steps and a fringe of metal railings. A plaque added at its foot records a bombing raid on 20 May 1941 which tragically killed nine villagers. The stone wall to the car park on the right belongs to the working men's club of 1899.

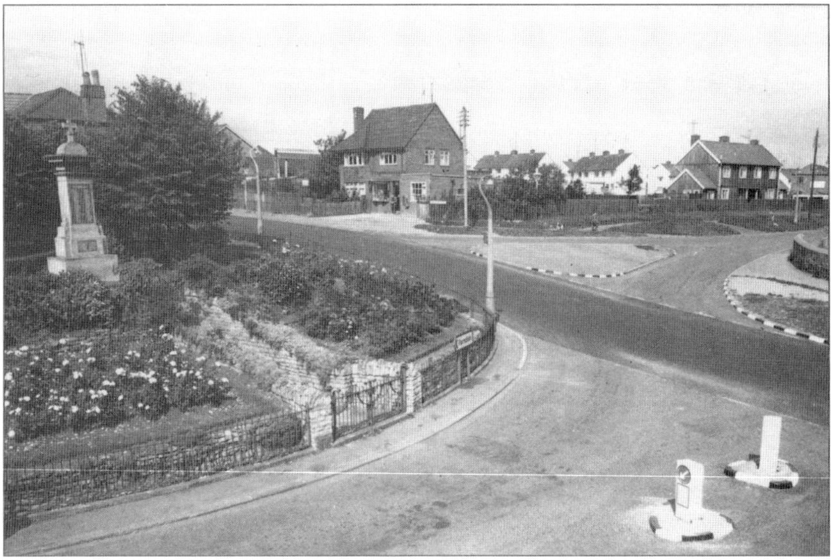

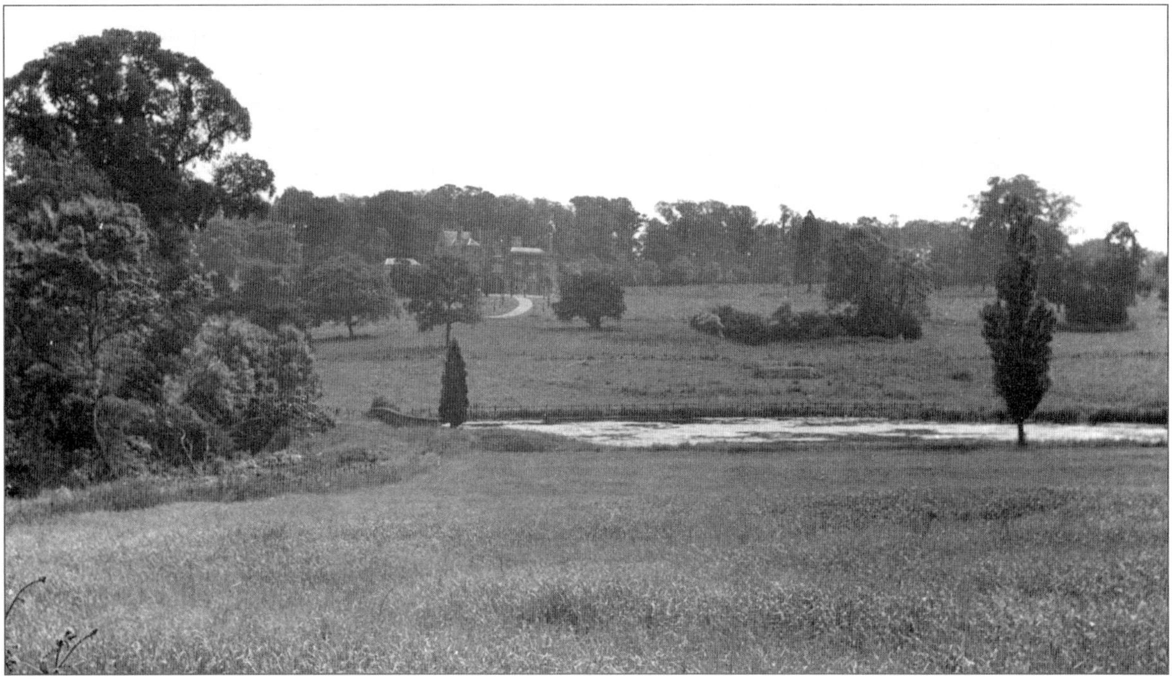

IRCHESTER, *Knuston Hall c1955* I71011

The route now heads east towards Rushden along the Irchester Road and passes Knuston Hall, which is situated in a delightful parkland setting complete with a lake formed by damming a stream that eventually reaches the Nene to the north. The stone mansion has 17th-, 18th- and 19th-century elements, and has long been owned by Northamptonshire County Council. It is now Knuston Hall Conference Centre and College of Adult Education, and well known for its thatching courses.

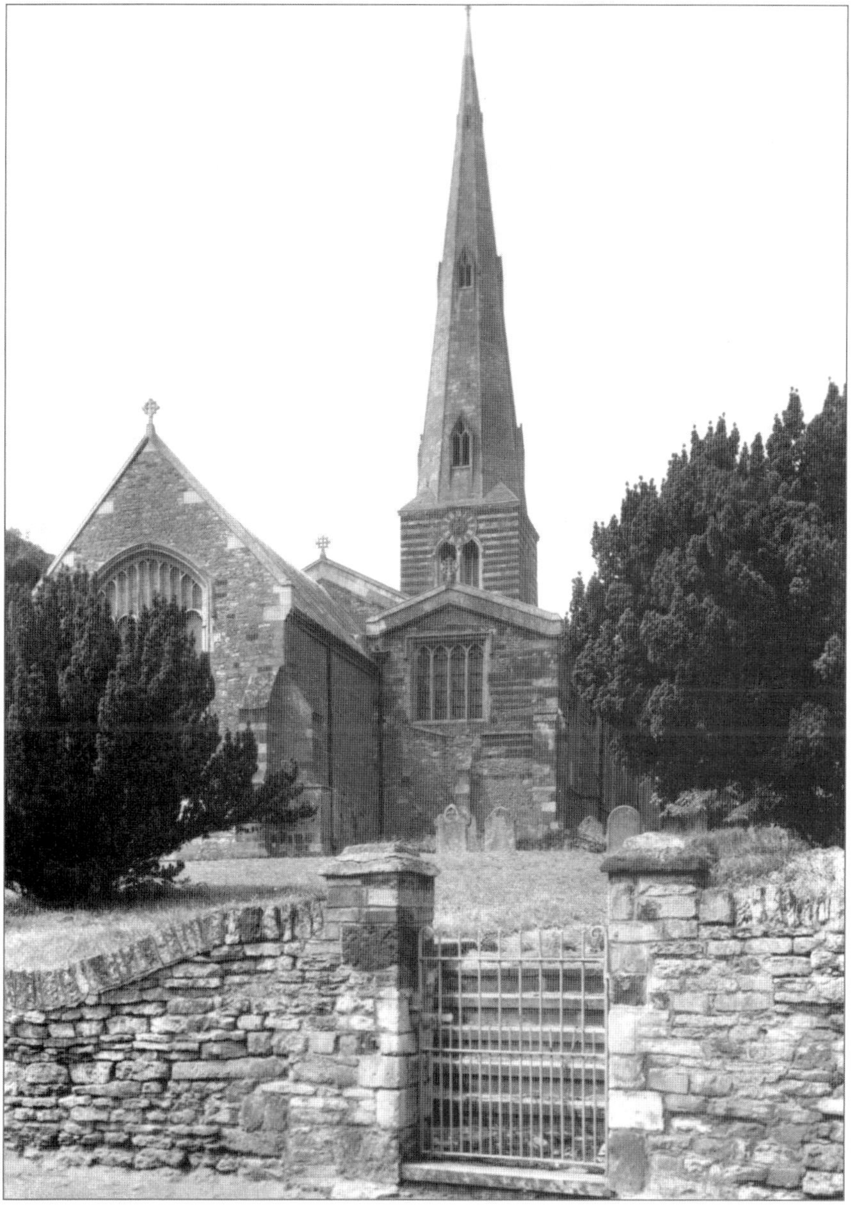

IRCHESTER, *The Parish Church c1955* I71014

The old village is in effect a small northern appendage to the much larger Victorian and later expansion. Irchester's fine banded ironstone and paler limestone church has a most elegant late 13th-century spire, but the churchyard wall has been rebuilt since the 1950s, in stone but less attractively. Nearer the river, and separated from the village by a belt of former ironstone quarries, was a Roman town; the clue to its existence is given by the Anglo-Saxon 'chester' element of the place name, a corruption of the Latin for fort, 'castra'.

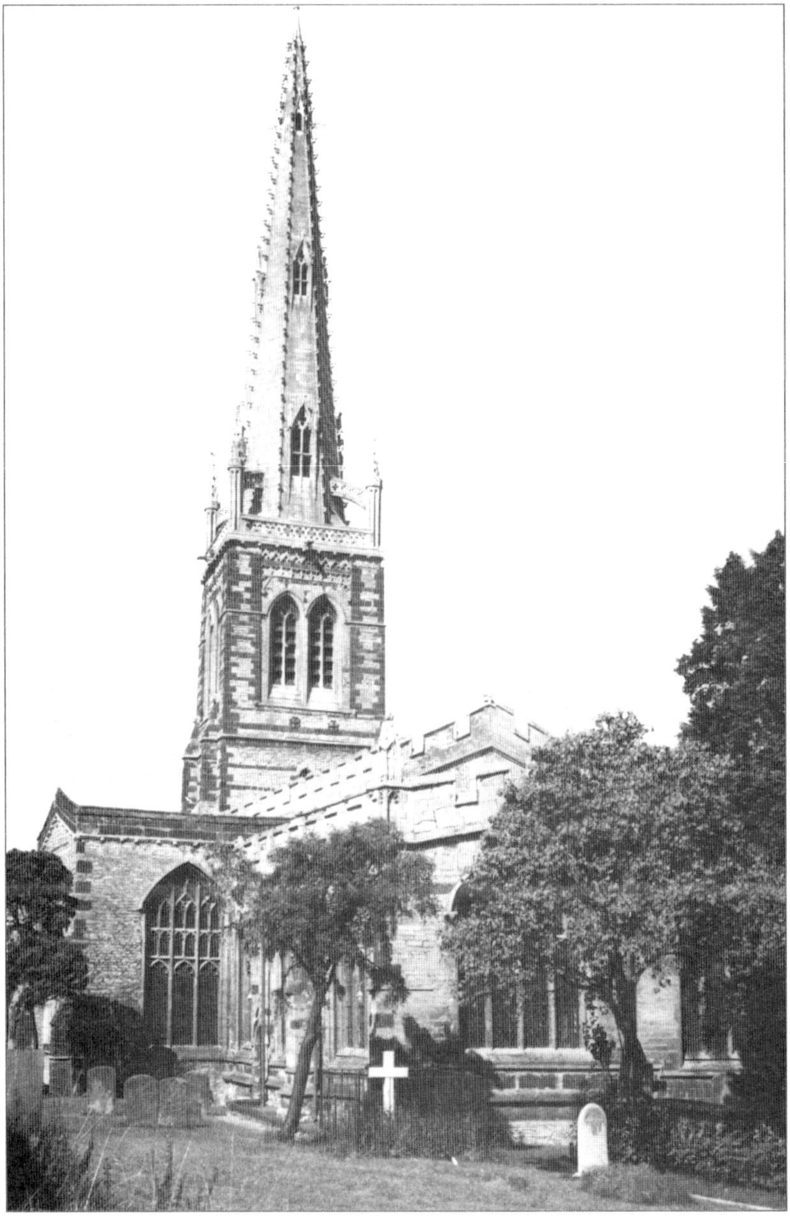

RUSHDEN, *The Parish Church c1955* R223019

From the rural splendour of Knuston Hall in its parkland the tour moves deep into boot and shoe country, starting at Rushden, a small town with a superb medieval church in its higher churchyard to the south of the High Street. Its dominance is emphasised by the tall tower and crocket-fringed spire: the weathervane perches over 165 feet above ground. What a pity that the town is no longer architecturally worthy of this fine Perpendicular Gothic masterpiece.

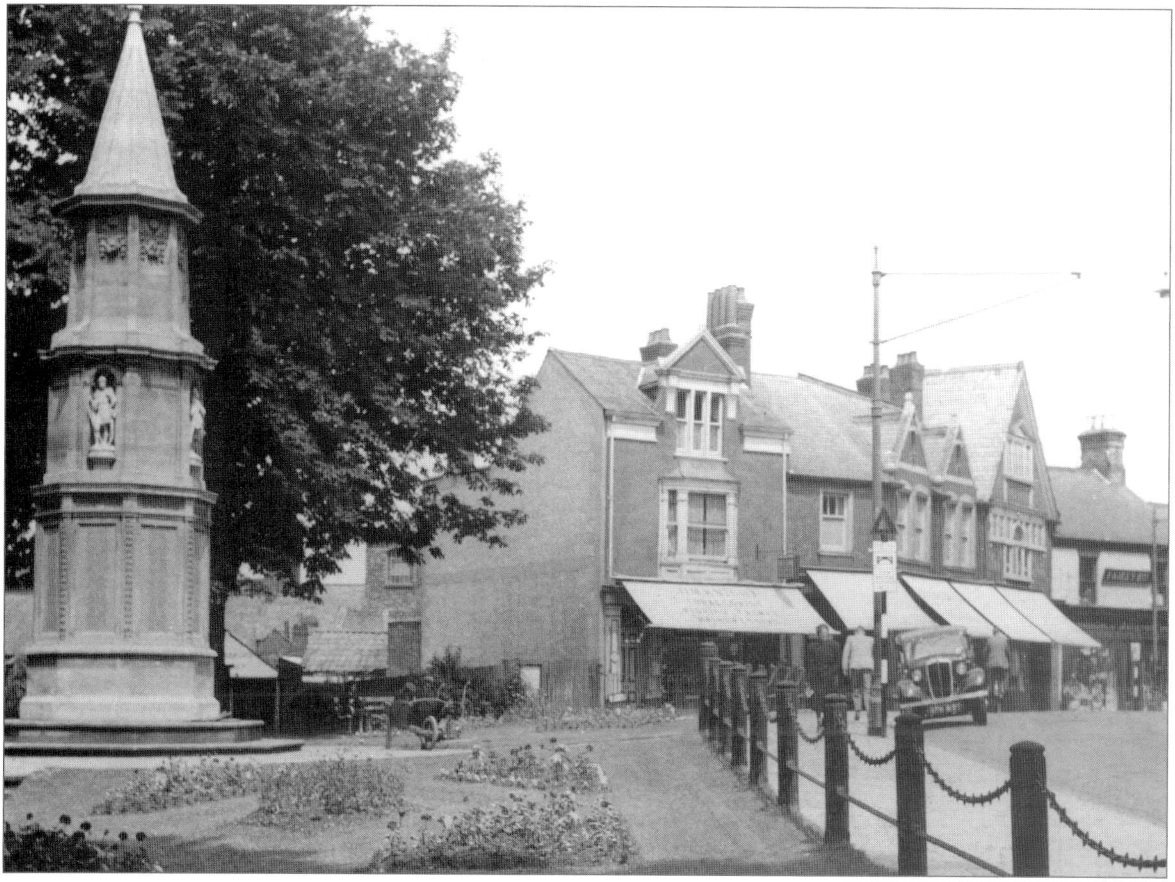

RUSHDEN
The War Memorial and High Street c1955 R223004

The town, originally noted for lace making, grew greatly in the 19th century, terraces and semis spilling out into the former open fields which had been enclosed in 1778. These terraces provided housing for the boot and shoe workers who were needed to service about 100 shoe factories that grew up in the town. Many Rushden men fell in World War I, and this unusual octagonal war memorial commemorates them in a small green at the junction of High Street and Skimmers Hill. The shops beyond have been merged into Peter Crisp's department store and brutally re-worked (2002).

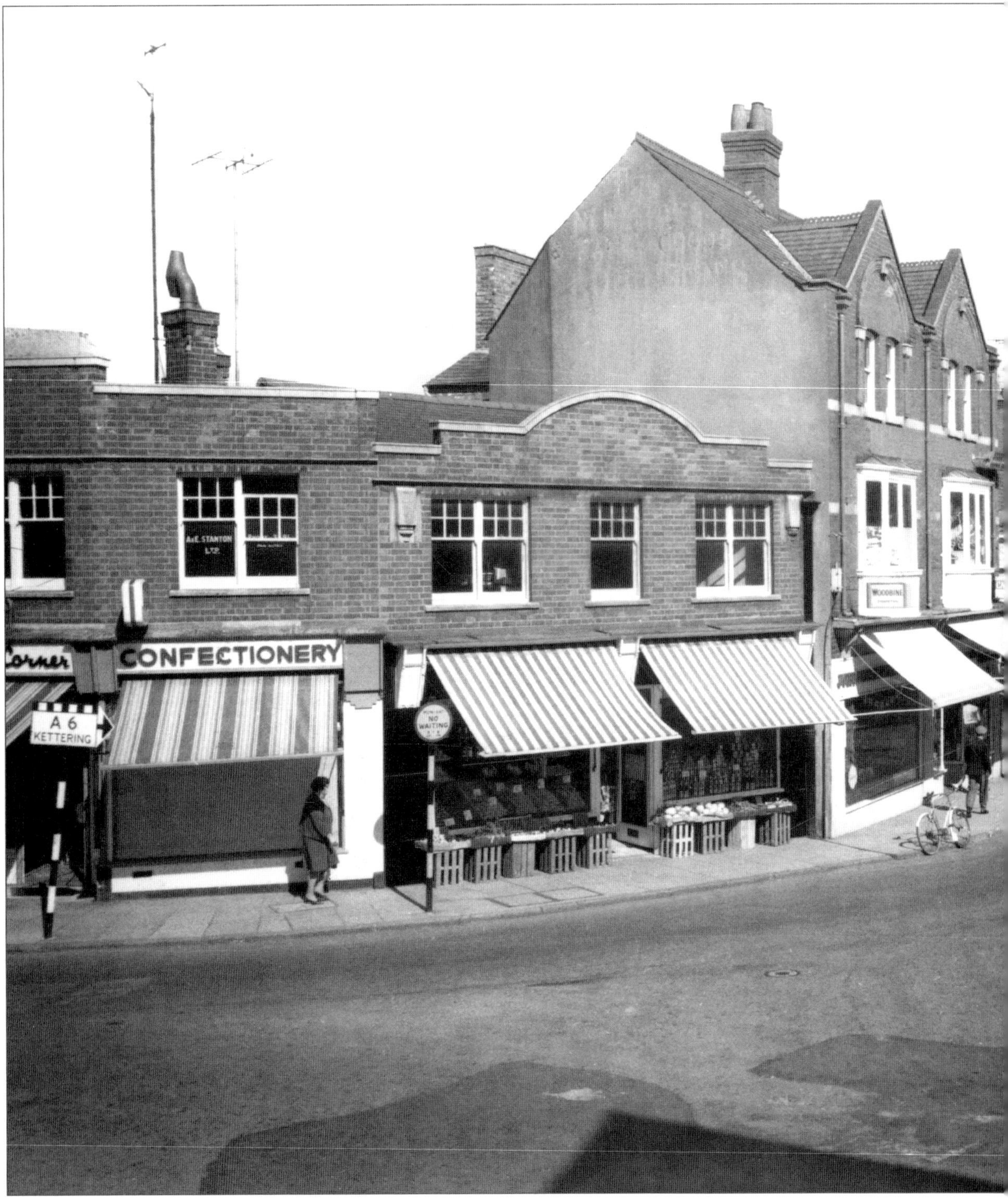
Corner
CONFECTIONERY
A 6
KETTERING
NO WAITING

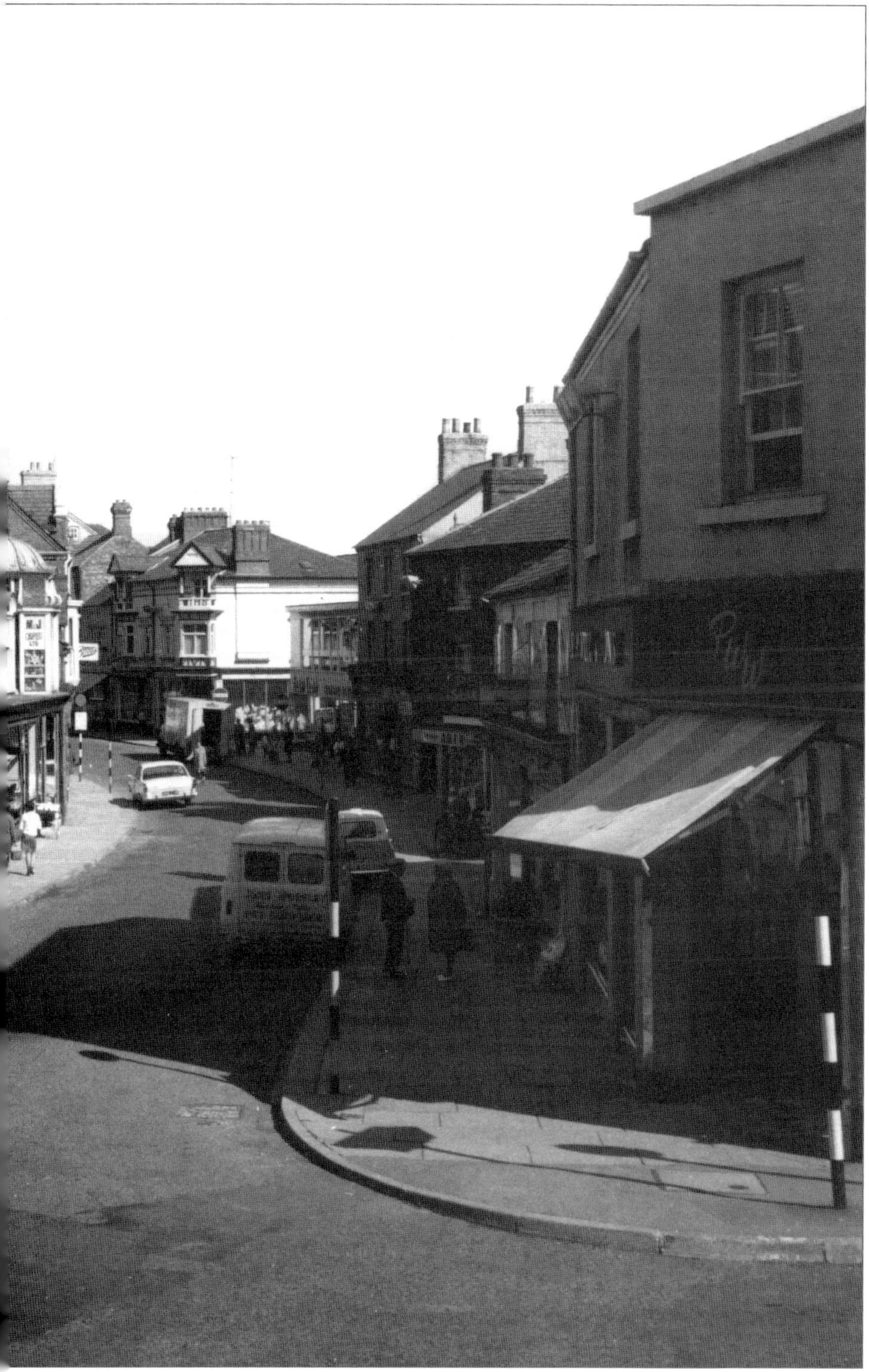

RUSHDEN
High Street c1955 R223021

Rushden's High Street could hardly be described as one of the better ones in Northamptonshire. Although there are a few late 18th- and earlier 19th-century buildings, the predominant character is that of the town's economic height in the late Victorian decades. The tall two-gabled building on the left is the Rushden Industrial Co-operative Society shop, founded in 1878 and rebuilt in the 1890s, and in the distance the chimneys belong to a rather grand Nat West bank of 1880.

RUSHDEN

The Hall c1955 R223002

To the west of High Street South and set in 18th-century landscaped parkland is the town's best building after the church: Rushden Hall. The park is now somewhat municipalized, but at its heart is the 17th-century stone-built hall with 19th-century wings and a walled former kitchen garden. The main front is round the right-hand corner; the porch is 19th-century. Rescued by the council, Rushden Hall was restored in 1970 and is now Rushden Town Council's offices, having again been restored in 1981.

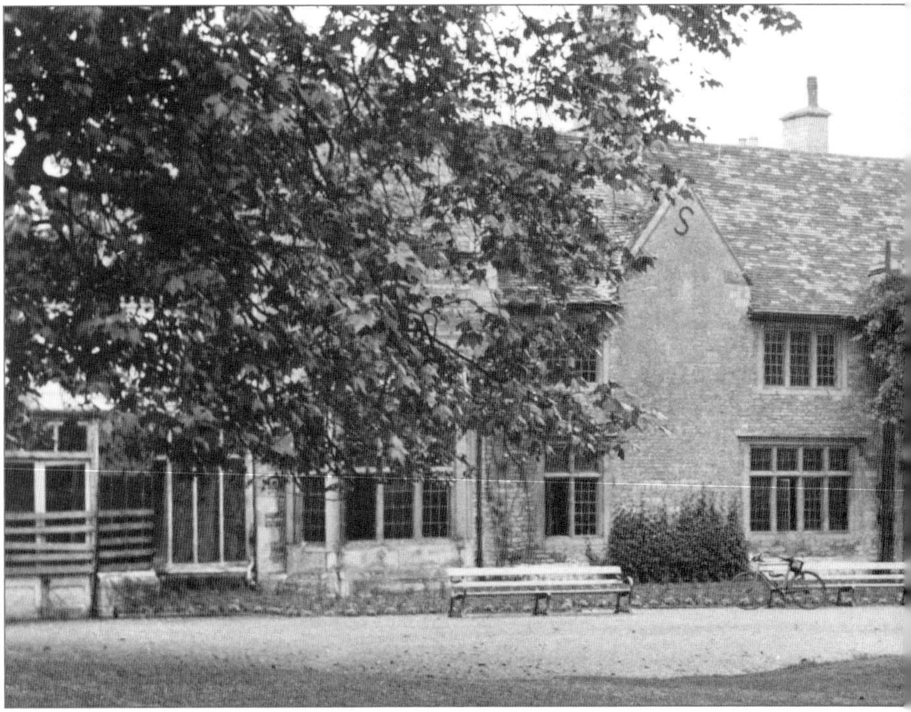

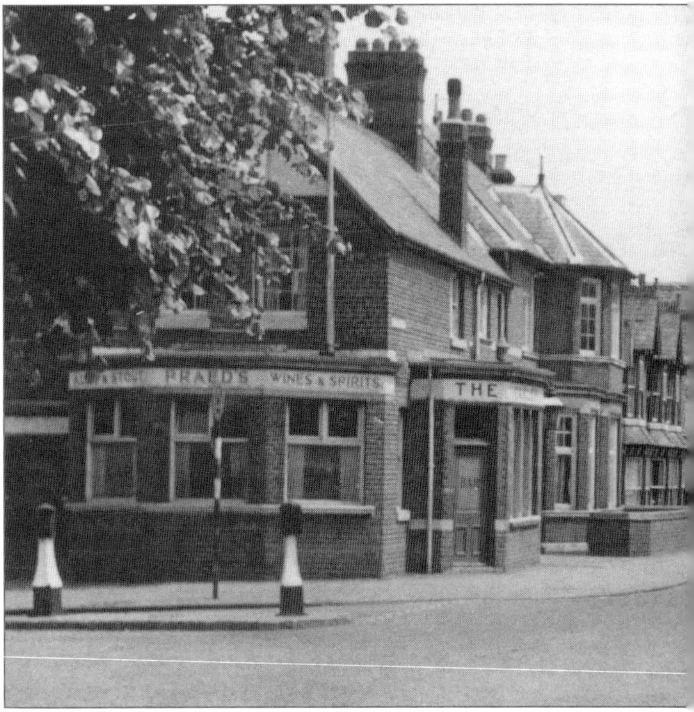

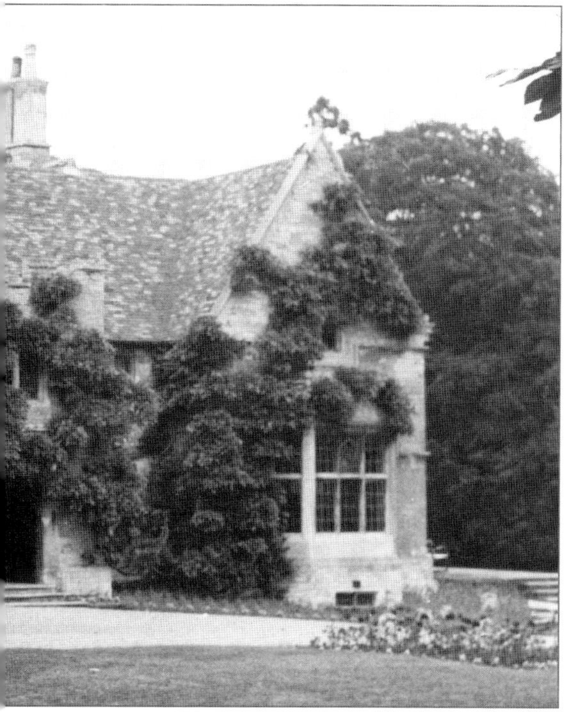

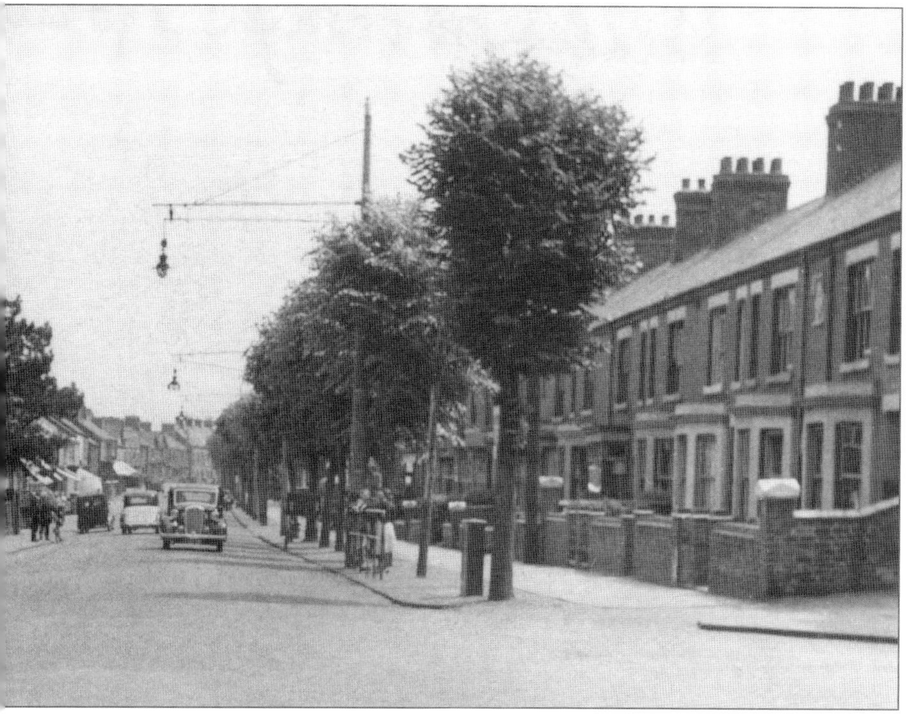

◀ **RUSHDEN**
Wellingborough Road c1955 R223009

Down Skimmers Hill, away from the church and Rushden Hall, Frith's photographer looks south-east back towards the town from the junction with Washbrook and Irchester Roads. On the left is The Oakley Arms, built in 1896 by Praed's brewery of Wellingborough, with a terrace of 1888 beyond; Lovell's Buildings opposite date from 1893, built for boot and shoe workers in hard red Midland brick. This 1950s view is still that of a shoe town, for in that decade 44% of the population still worked in the trade.

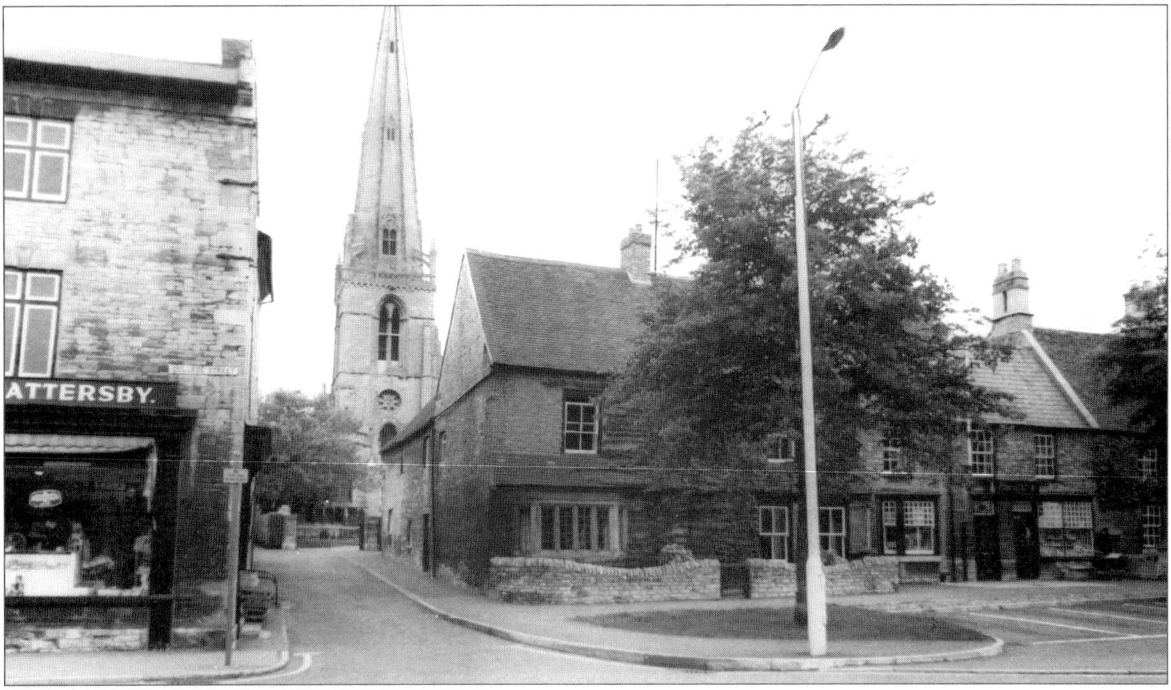

▲ **HIGHAM FERRERS**
The Parish Church c1965 H245036

Rushden merges north into Higham Ferrers, a town with a much more distinguished history. It had a market before 1086, although a formal market charter was only granted in 1251, and a Norman castle, of which only ditches and part of the moat survive. At the town's heart is the triangular market place surrounded by good buildings, mostly 17th-century and Georgian. This view looks down the lane towards the superb church, mostly 13th-century with a 14th-century spire.

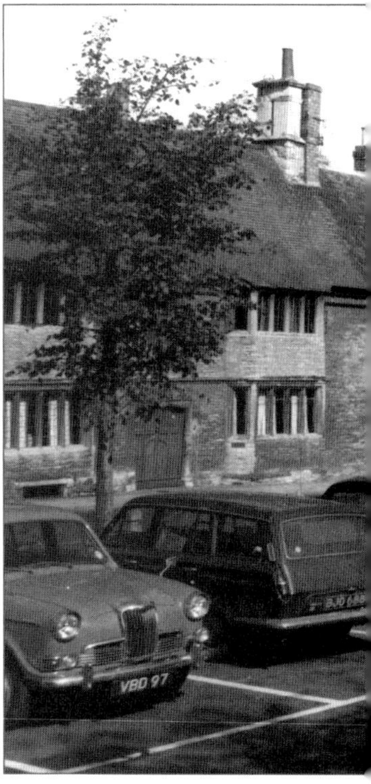

▶ **HIGHAM FERRERS**
Market Square c1965 H245028

This view looks northwards, with the 1809 Town Hall behind Frith's photographer, towards the 14th-century market cross on its later conical rubble-stone mound which replaced a more usual stepped base. While still a car park, the spaces have now been marked out more sensitively by setts, rather than white lines. Note the 17th-century stone bay windows to the house on the left.

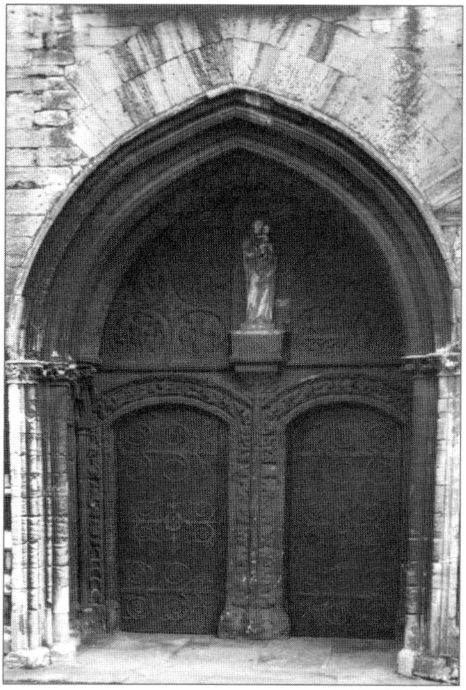

HIGHAM FERRERS

The Parish Church, the West Door c1955 H245014

Visitors could be forgiven for thinking they were in 13th-century France when they reach the quite outstanding west doorway in the tower front. The master mason was probably close to the court of Henry III, who was at the time rebuilding Westminster Abbey. The segmental door arches are distinctly French Gothic, and so are the figures in the jambs and the biblical scenes below the outer arch. The Virgin and Child has now been replaced by a modern one, and the stonework has been cleaned.

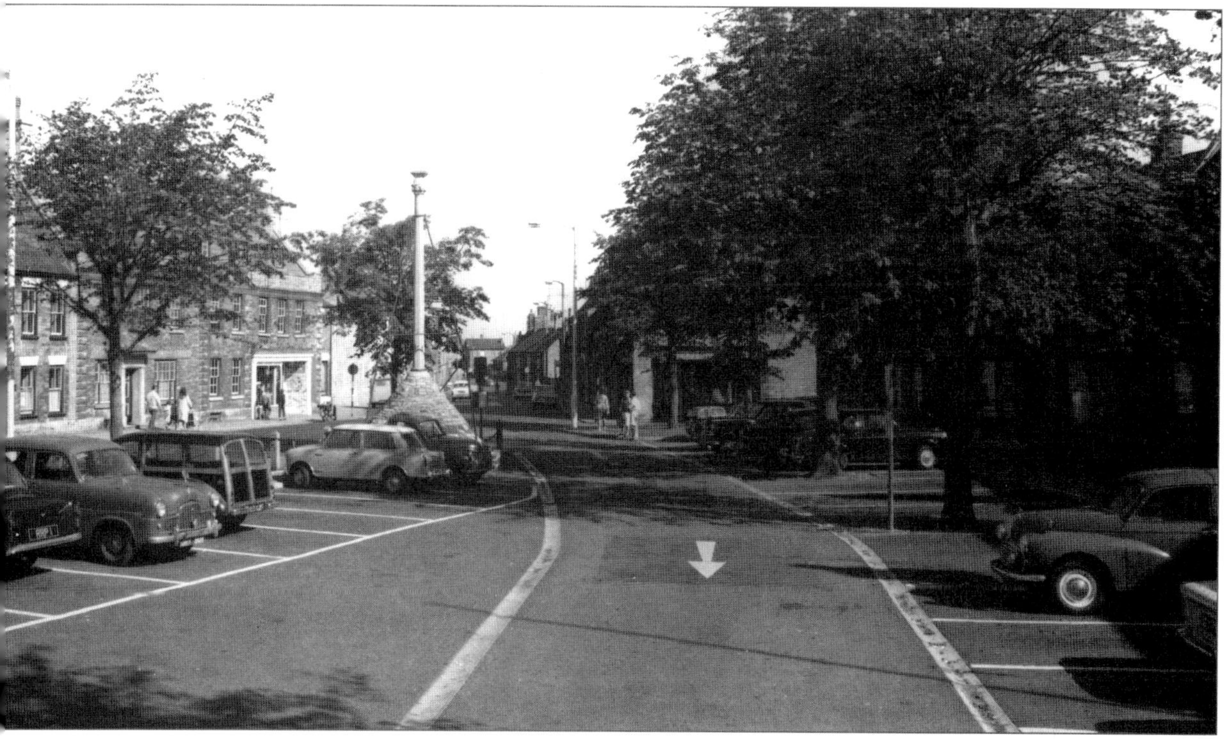

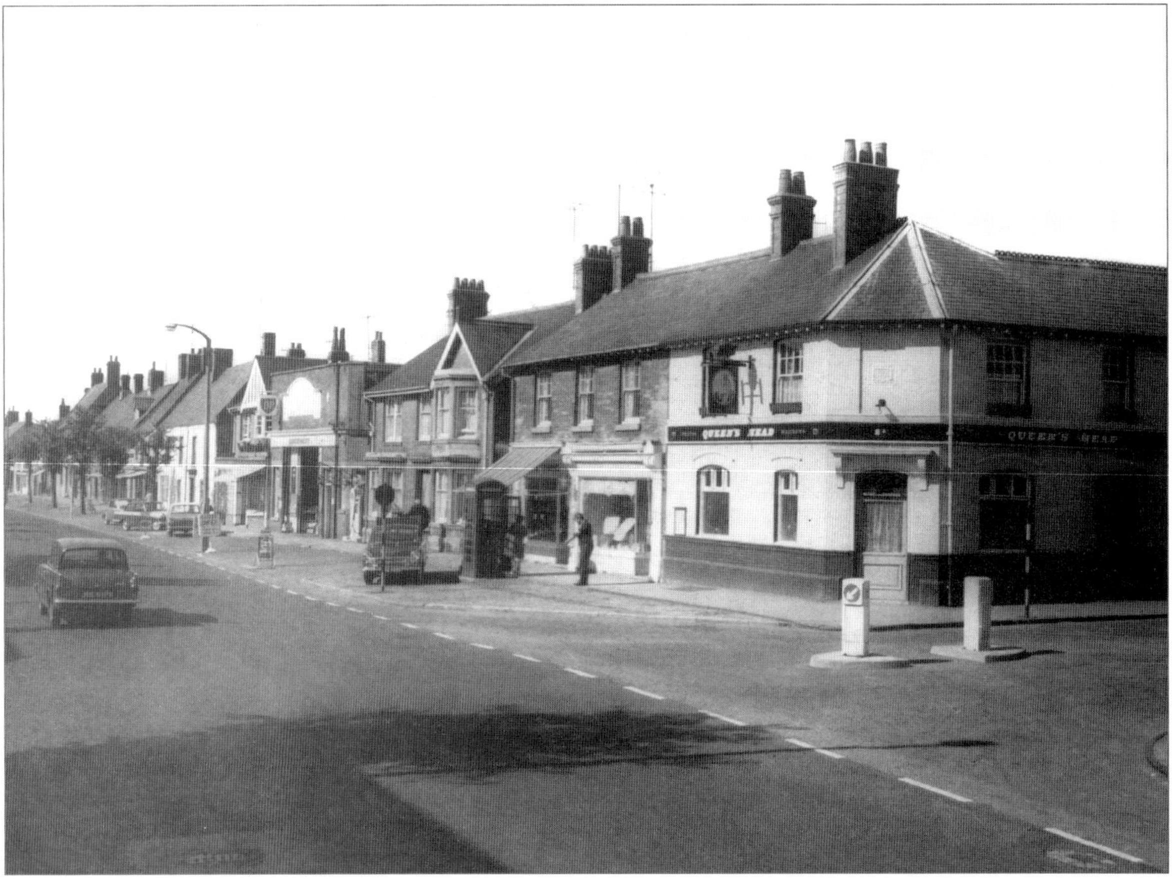

HIGHAM FERRERS, *High Street c1965* H245030

Frith's photographer now looks southwards from the Market Square into the High Street. The turning for Wharf Road is on the right, with the white painted Queen's Head pub of 1905 on the corner. Wharf Road, of course, led to now long-gone wharves along the River Nene half a mile away. The gabled building beyond the telephone kiosk, Rudlen House (centre), dates from 1911, while the BP garage beyond now sells cars.

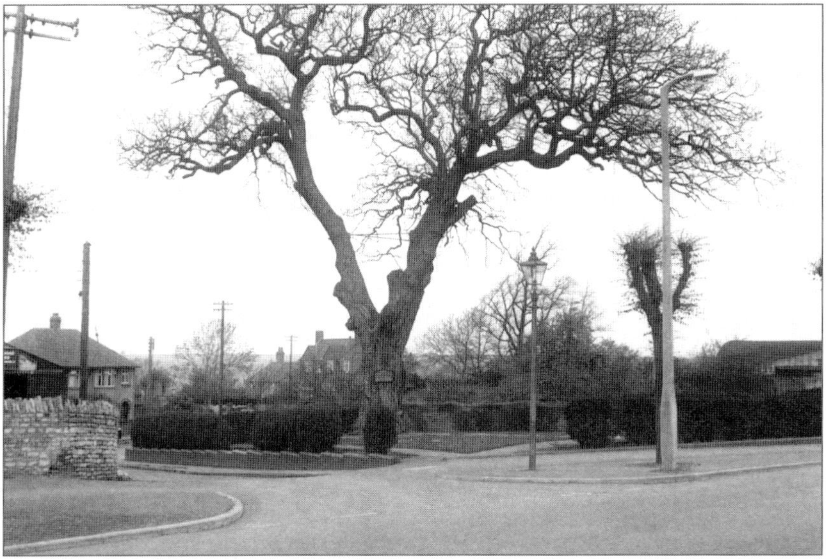

HIGHAM FERRERS
The Walnut Tree, North End c1955 H245005

Leaving the town northwards, our tour passes through North End. Here, at the Kings Meadow Lane turning, an ancient walnut tree sits in a small triangular hedged green. The walnut tree is reputed to be over 600 years old, as the now long-gone plaque hanging on it recorded. The works on the right have recently been demolished and are now being replaced (2003) by a vast housing estate called Lancaster Downs, named in honour of the Duchy of Lancaster, which has owned most of Higham since 1266.

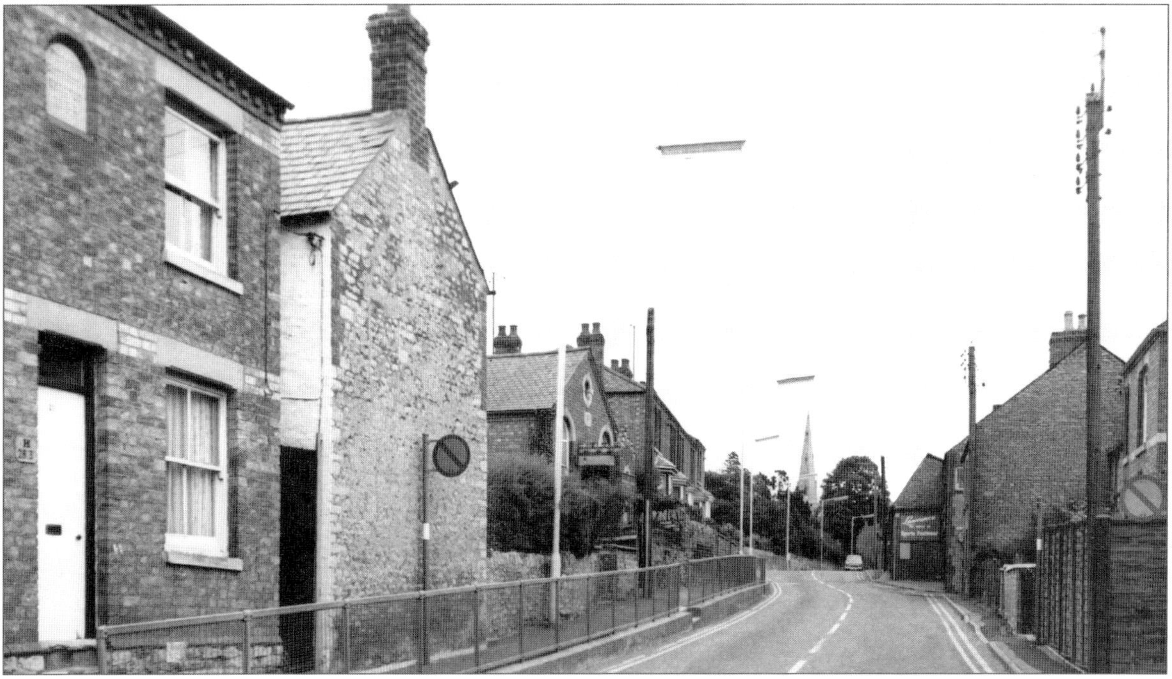

STANWICK, *West Street c1965* S628016

From Higham Ferrers the route continues north-east along the edge of the Nene valley to Stanwick, a village that remains relatively small, unlike Raunds to its north-east. This view looks east along West Street towards the older village centre up the hill. This part, though, is mostly 19th-century: Pitham Cottage on the left is dated 1884, and the Methodist church beyond with the round window in the gable was built in 1895. Since the 1960s, some houses on the right have been demolished for Samuels Close.

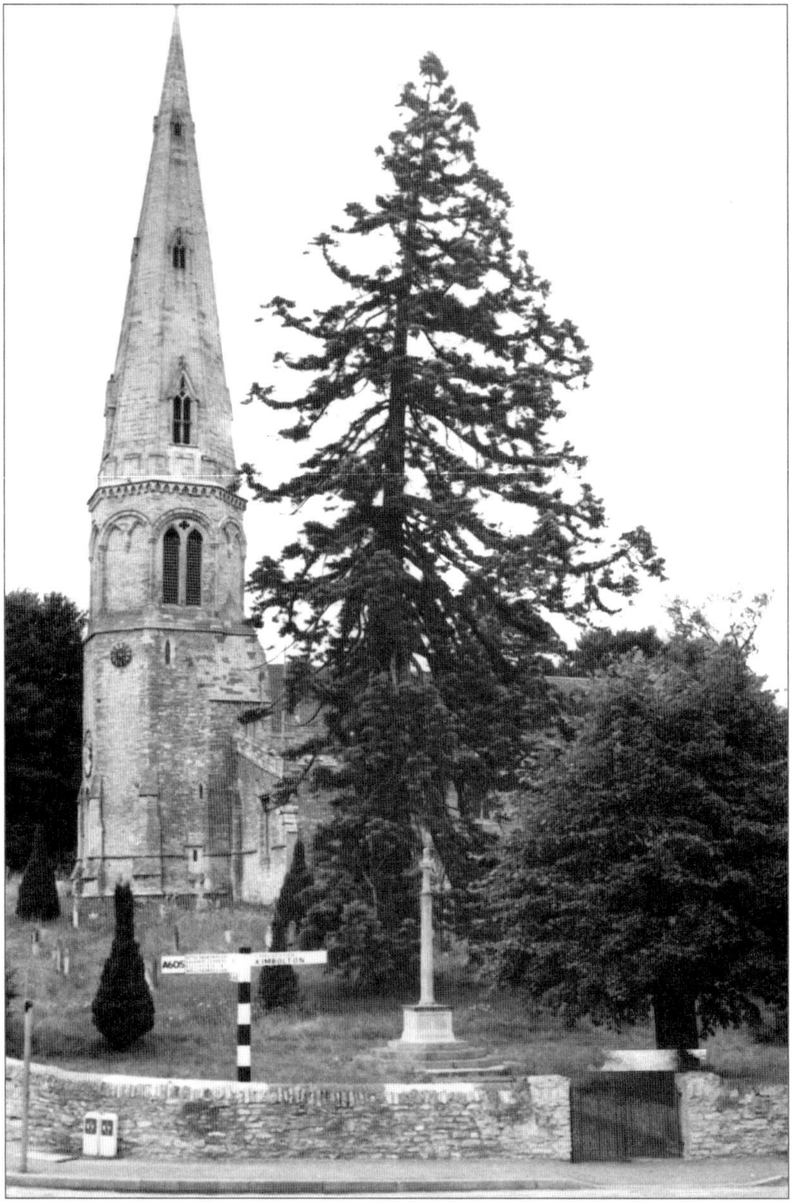

STANWICK, *The Parish Church c1960* S628002

In the village centre the parish church of St Lawrence has a most unusual octagonal tower of the13th century surmounted by the more usual octagonal spire, reaching a total height of 155 feet. To the right, just out of view in Church Street, is The Duke of Wellington pub, a stone building mostly of the 18th and early 19th century; it commemorates the first Wellington boots, which were made for the duke in a Stanwick boot maker's.

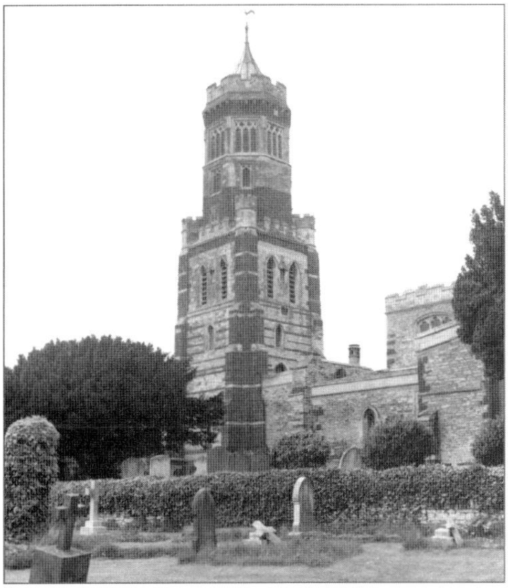

IRTHLINGBOROUGH
St Peter's Parish Church c1969 I33013

The parish church lies south of the High Street and the market cross. The rather curious church tower is conventional to the belfry stage, but then instead of a spire it has a two-storey octagonal upper tower. The effect is heightened by the use of the brown ironstone and the grey limestone. The tower, started around 1354 or 1380, had to be rebuilt in the 1880s.

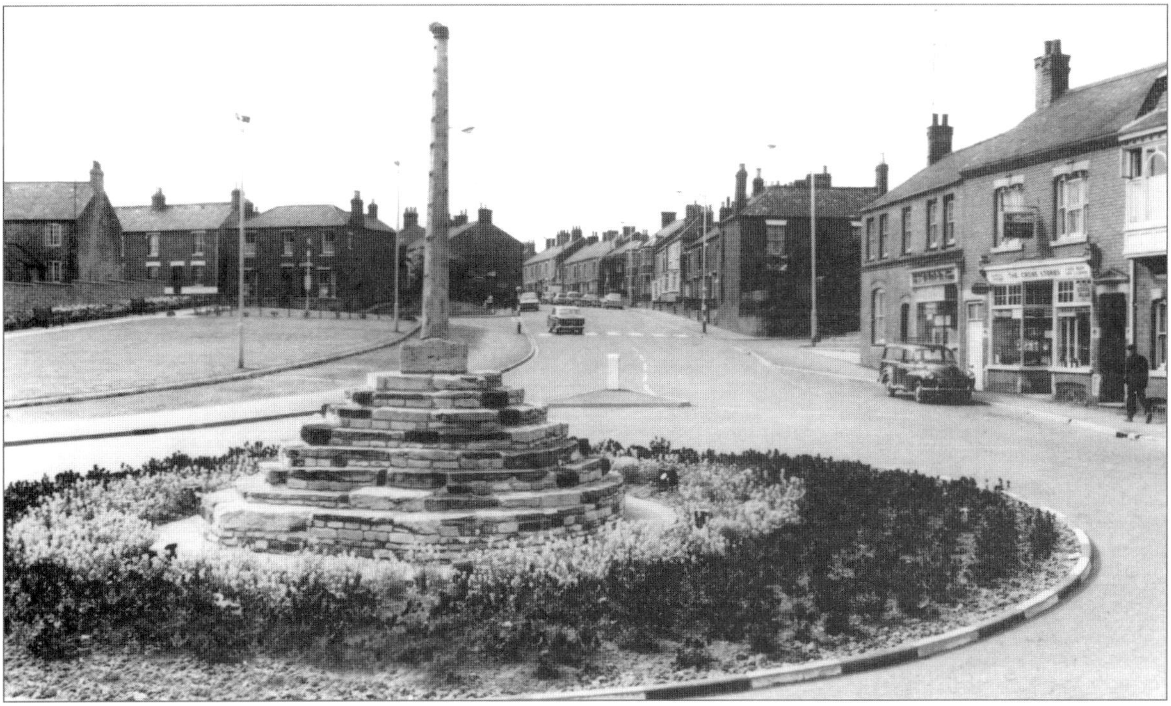

IRTHLINGBOROUGH, *The Cross c1965* I33015

The lane leading from the church meets the junction of the High Street, Finedon Road and Station Road, with the medieval market cross on its eight-step base occupying a small roundabout. Since the 1960s the flowers have been replaced by grass. The cross is a reminder that this industrial town is ancient, having been a market town since before 1100. The rest of the buildings in this view greatly post-date the cross, being mostly late 19th-century.

IRTHLINGBOROUGH
High Street 1969 I33021

The High Street is a disappointment after the fine church and the medieval market cross. Its heart has been punched out, and the lost buildings have been replaced by the dullness of the shopping parade on the right and of the Co-op on the left (now a Tesco Express). Irthlingborough was, like Rushden, an important boot and shoe manufacturing town, but in 1969 the industry was already in decline through cheap foreign imports. In the distance is the spike of the Market Cross.

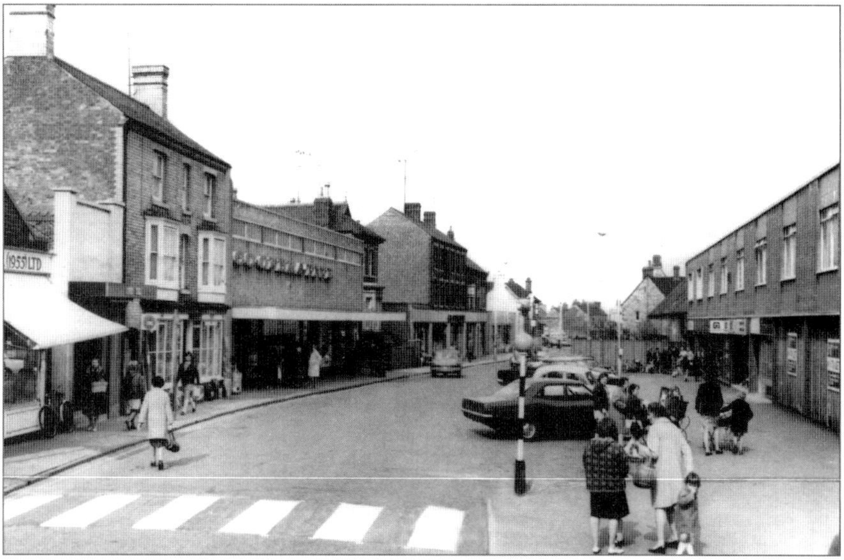

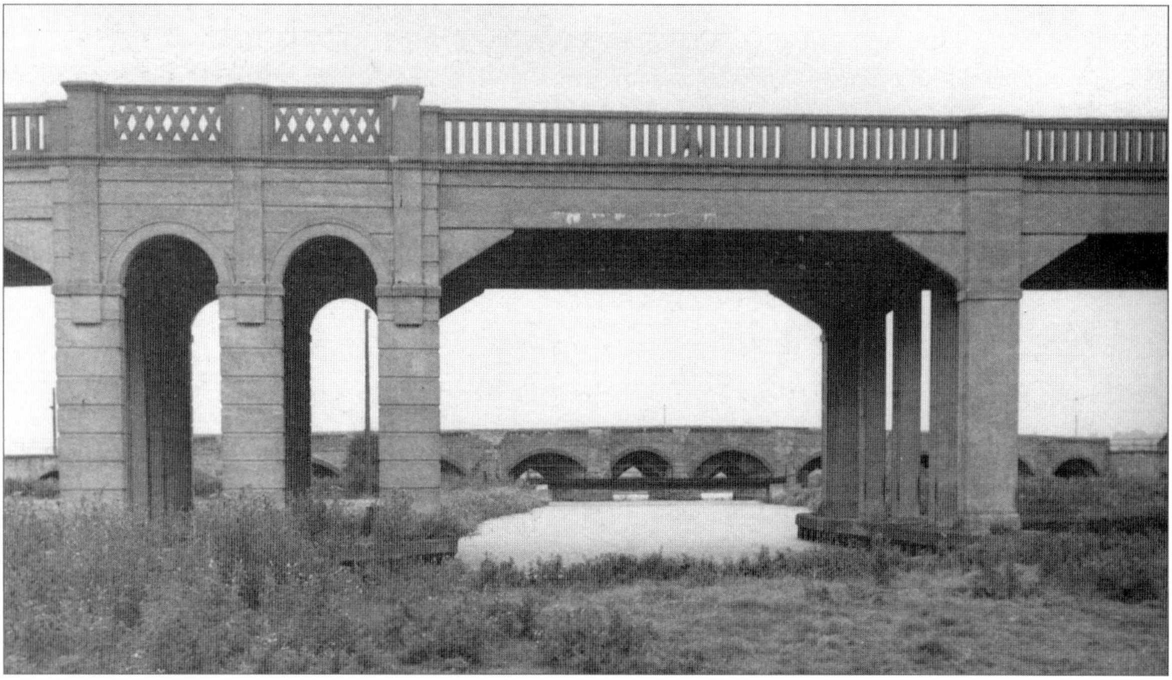

IRTHLINGBOROUGH, *The Nene Bridges c1960* I33005

To the east of the town the A61, the Kettering to Higham Ferrers road, crosses the River Nene. Until 1922 it crossed on a narrow 14th-century stone bridge of ten arches. This was widened in 1922. Clearly this was not enough to cope with increased traffic, and the high reinforced concrete bridge in the foreground now carries the main road. Out of view to the left is the stadium of the Rushden and Diamonds football club, which achieved promotion to Division 3 of the Football League in 2001.

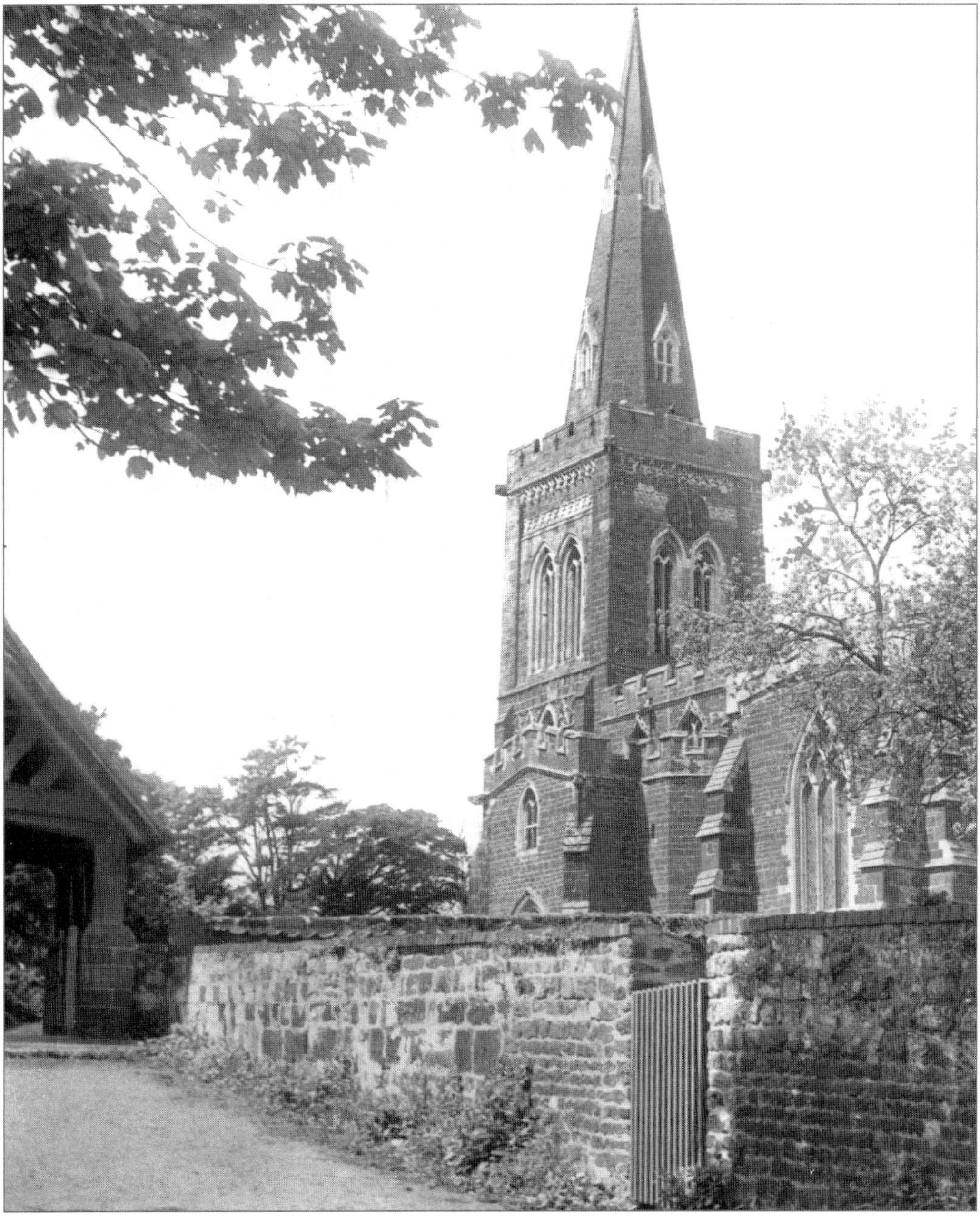

FINEDON, *The Parish Church c1955* F184010

Moving on, we reach Finedon village, passing its well known ornate brick water tower of 1904 on the Irthlingborough road. This is another boot and shoe village that expanded greatly in the 19th century, but it has a core of older ironstone buildings at its west end near the church and Finedon Hall. There were also iron-working quarries which had their own branch railway, but this ceased in 1946. Beyond the 1886 lychgate, the fine parish church is mostly 14th-century with an elegant recessed spire.

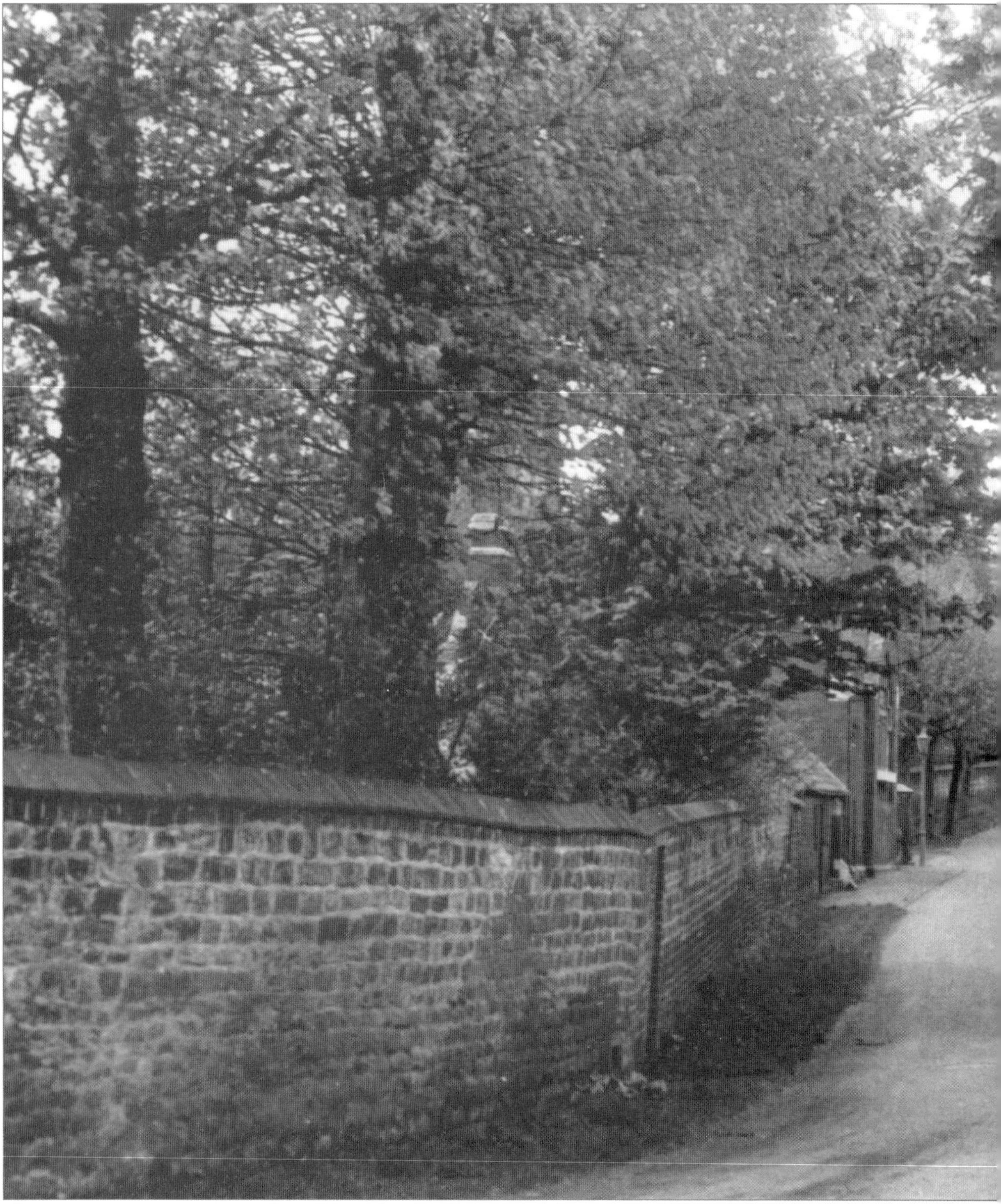

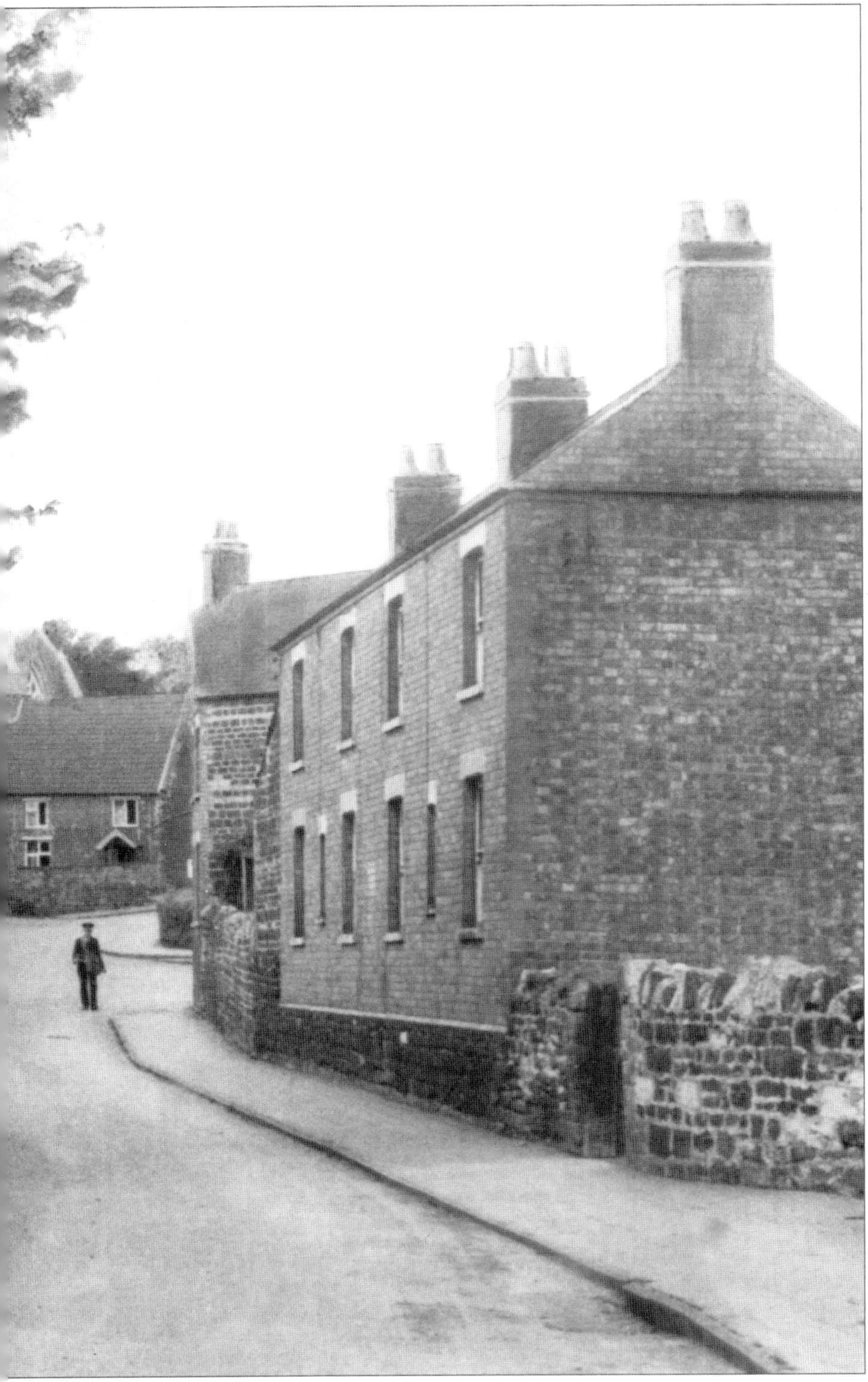

FINEDON
Lime Tree End c1955
F184005

A little further down Church Hill, in Lime Tree End, this view is of the older part of the village. In medieval times Finedon was a market town with a market dating back to before 1294. The lime trees remain, but road improvement in the 1960s demolished the houses on the right, replacing them with a small green. The house opposite the postman on his rounds (centre) is Thingdon Cottage, built in 1862 by the eccentric lord of the manor, William Mackworth-Dolben (Thingdon is the older name for Finedon).

FINEDON
The War Memorial c1960
F184014

The other two views in Finedon show the Victorian area of the village that spans the Wellingborough road, a distinctly different architectural style. This view looks past the war memorial in its railed and hedged enclosure. The memorial bears a single uplifting word on each face: 'cheerfulness', 'prowess', 'courage' and 'endurance'. To the left are houses of 1891 and 1885. Opposite, 1950s shop buildings have appeared, including Wills in the lower flat-roofed one; this is still J Wills, an electrical store, in 2003, and the chemist still a chemist.

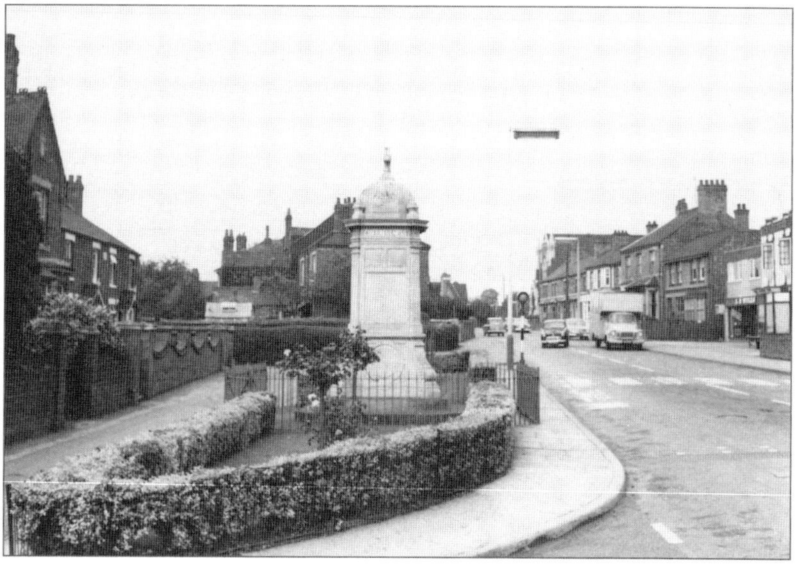

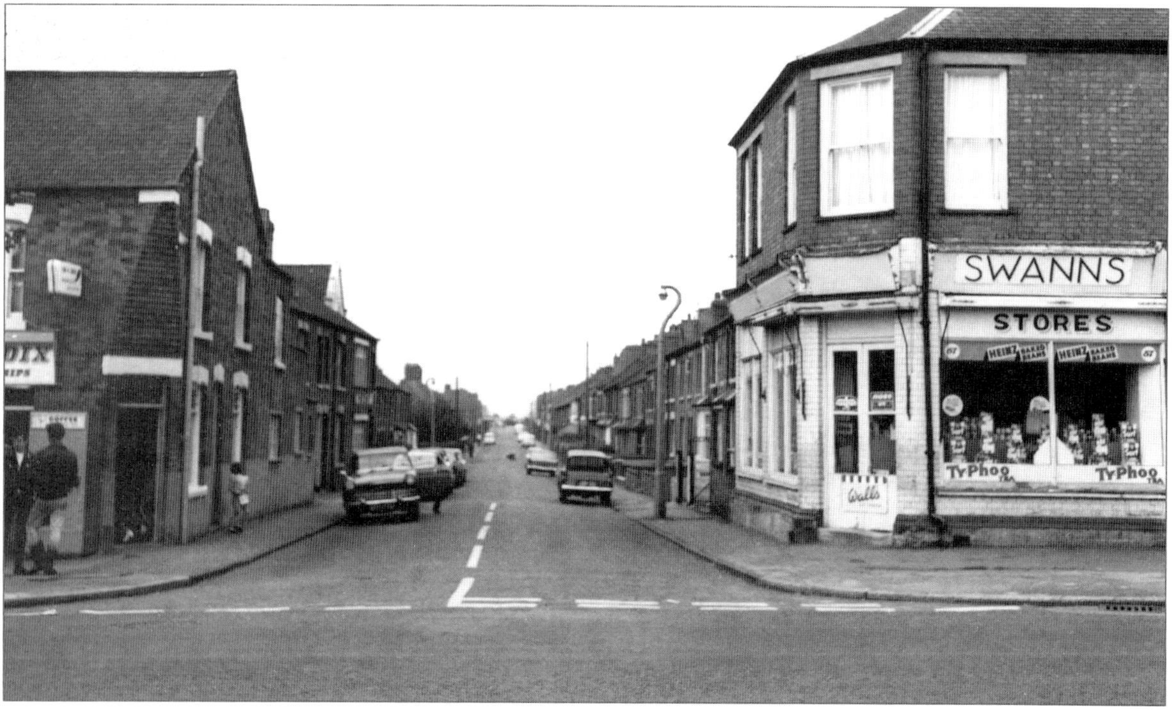

FINEDON, *Allen Road c1960* F184020

This view shows typical artisan terrace housing, seen from the Irthlingborough Road. Allen Road's terraces have small front gardens set out on a dead straight street. The fish and chip shop on the left-hand corner is now Tudor Fish and Chips and a Chinese food takeaway, while Swanns with its amateur sign is now D & A store, an off-licence and general store. It is good to see such continuity and the survival of small shops in a large village.

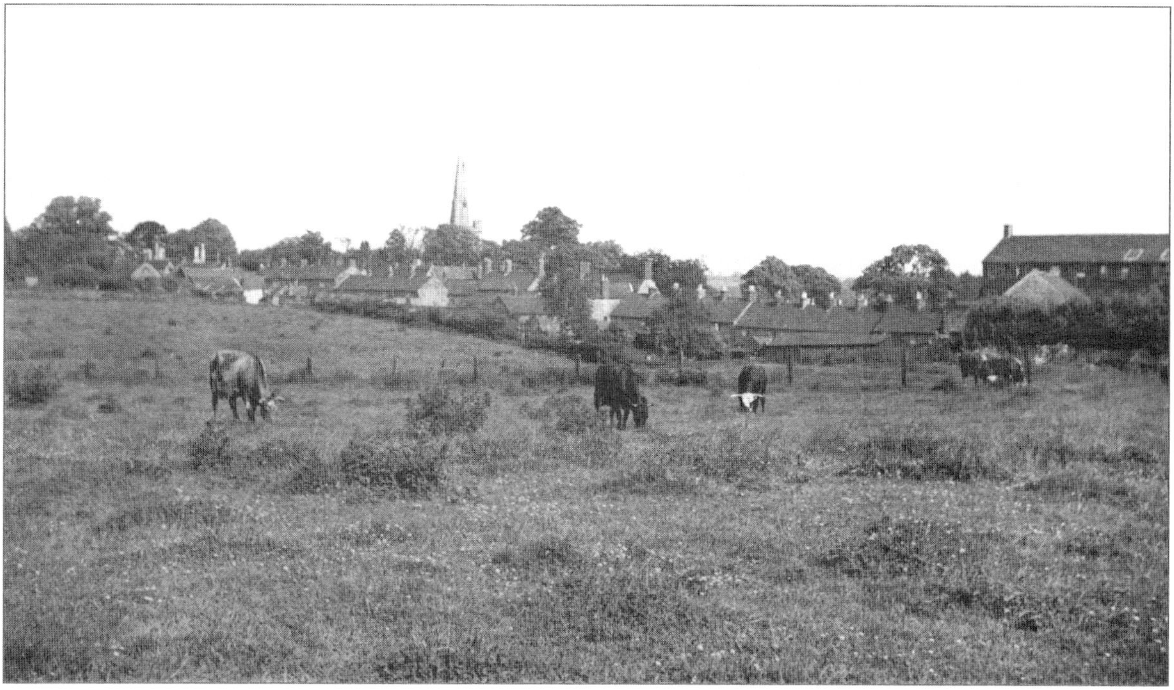

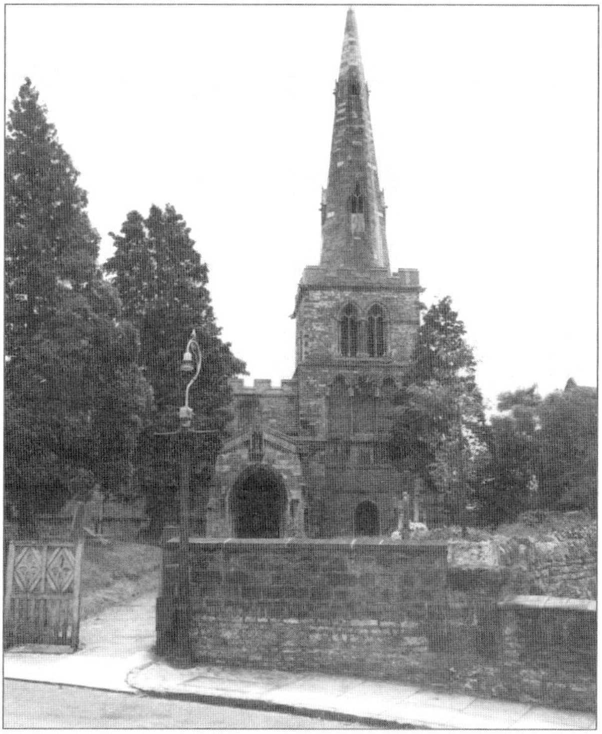

▲ **BURTON LATIMER**
From Kettering Road c1955 B390007

Burton Latimer had a pre-boot and shoe existence as a minor cotton-spinning village, followed by carpet and worsted weaving in the early 19th century; then the railway came, so key to many of the boot and shoe towns and villages. This view looks south-east over the village from beside the Kettering Road, with the grounds of the partly Jacobean Burton Latimer Hall behind the photographer and out of view. To the right is one of the shoe factories, now demolished, and to the left the spire of the parish church.

◄ **BURTON LATIMER**
The Parish Church c1965 B390014

Church Street contains some of the village's oldest houses and the pretty stone-built former school of 1622. The churchyard is now entered through an iron arch with a lantern and iron gates rather than the timber ones in this view. The tower was accurately rebuilt in 1866 and a new chancel was added in 1867. The tower was early 14th-century and surmounted by yet another Northamptonshire spire.

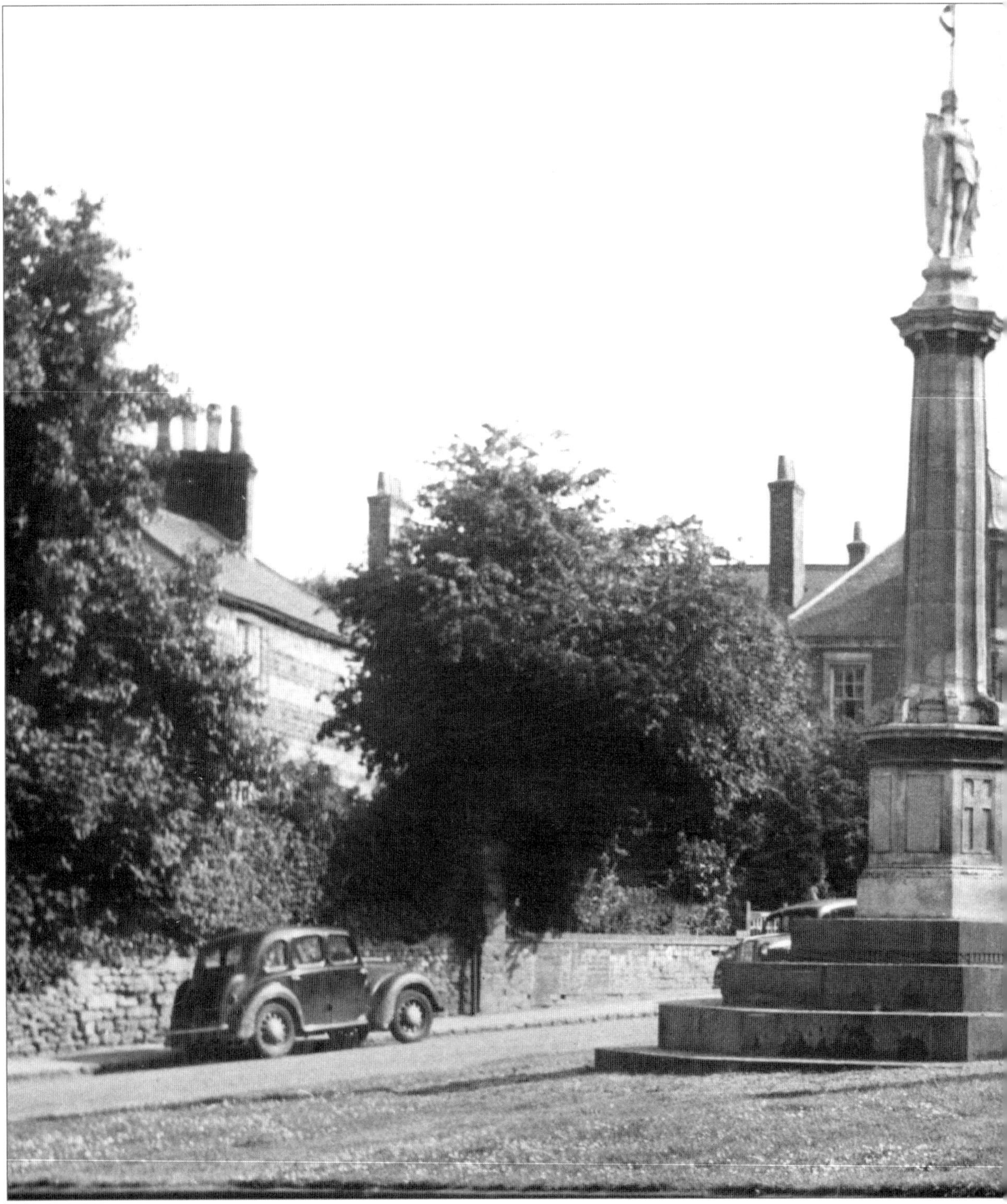

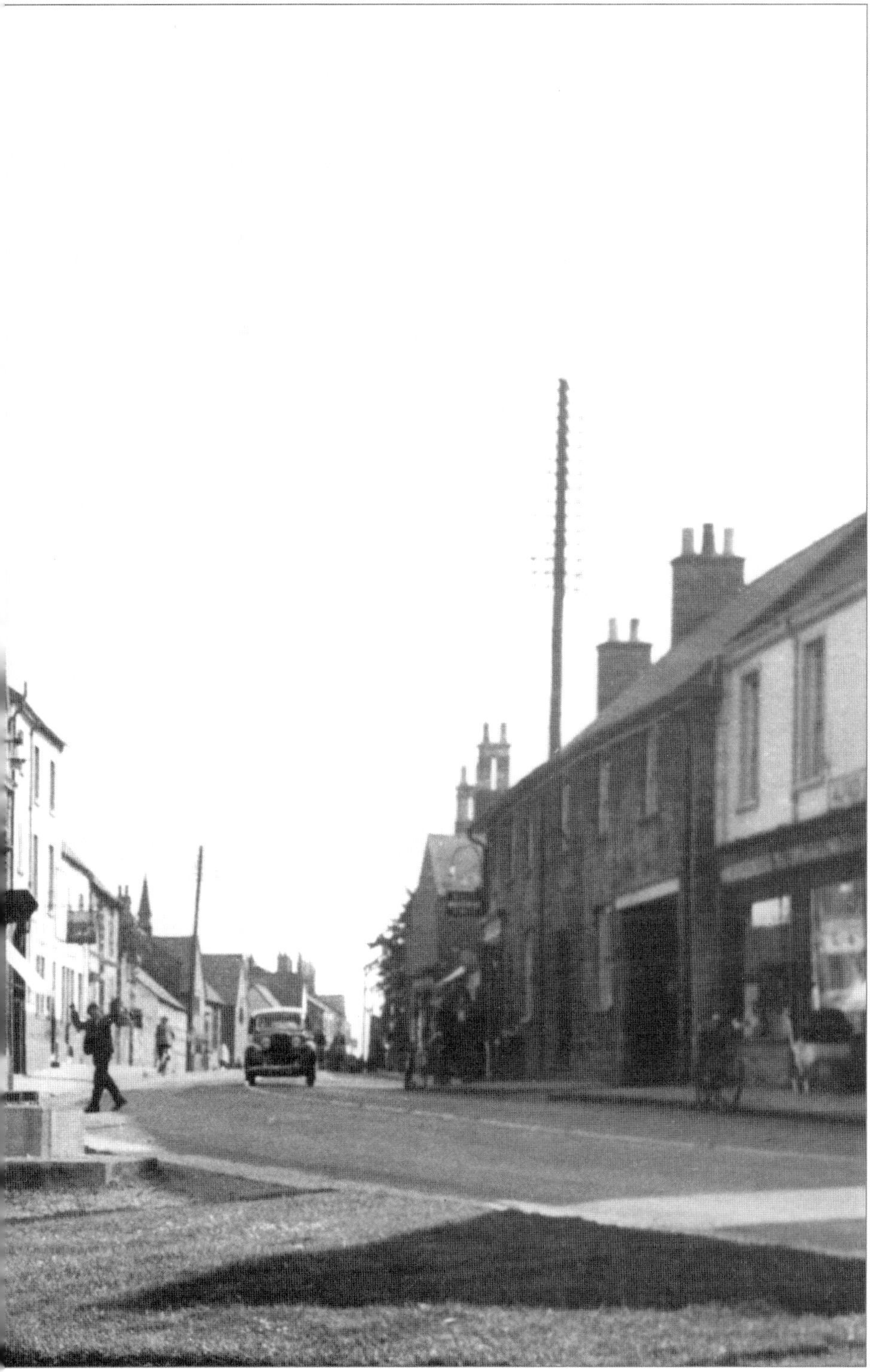

BURTON LATIMER
The War Memorial and the High Street c1955
B390005

The war memorial of the early 1920s was erected at the junction of Church Street with the High Street, its ornate column surmounted by Saint George. Soon after this view was taken, the memorial was dismantled and removed to the grounds of the Council Offices further down the High Street (view B390024 page 74). However, it was recently re-erected here on a slightly different location.

BURTON LATIMER
The Council Offices and the War Memorial c1965 B390024

This view shows the war memorial in its temporary home before relocation to its original site (view B390005 page 73). The early 20th-century building on the right became the council offices and is now the Kettering Borough Council's Burton Latimer District Office. The two trees survive.

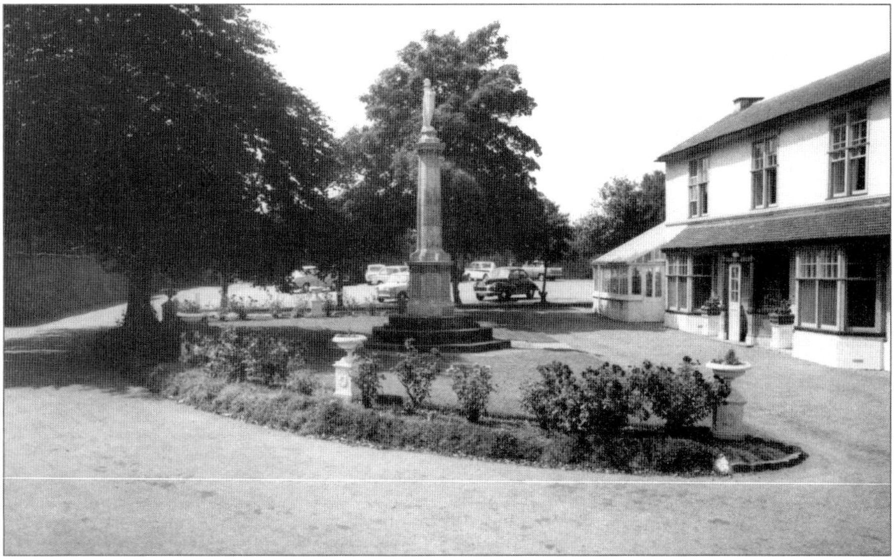

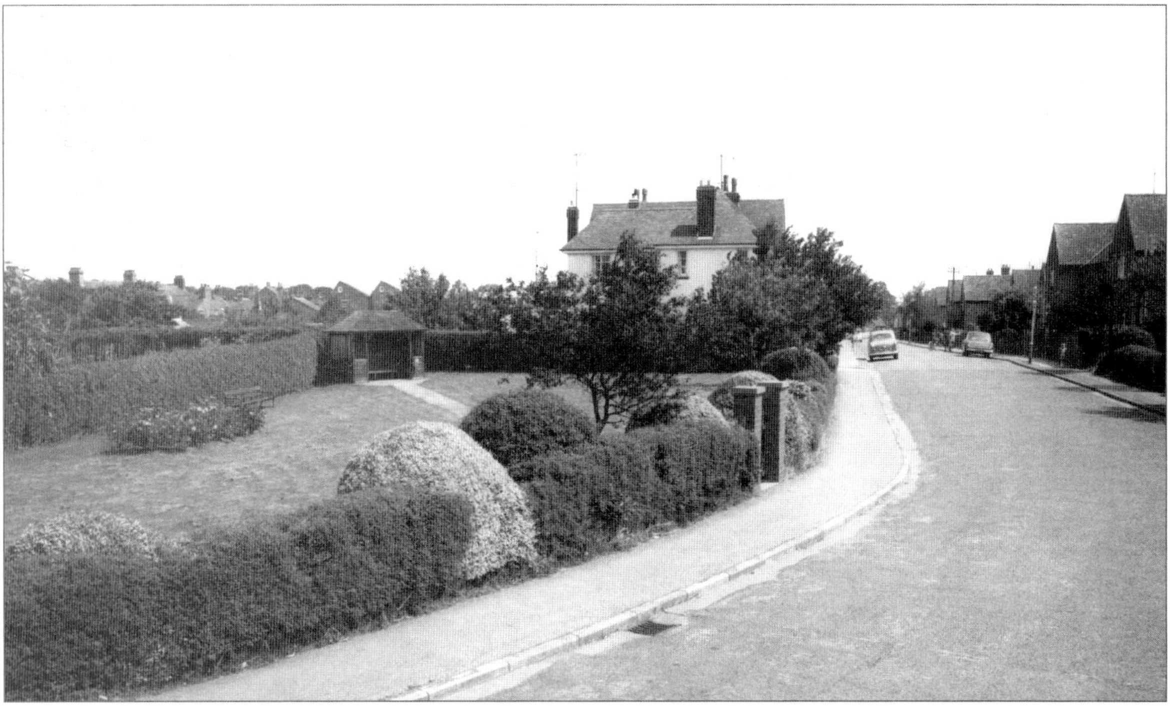

BURTON LATIMER, *Pioneer Avenue c1965* B390011

Pioneer Avenue runs west from the High Street with mostly late 19th-century and inter-war semi-detached houses. It passes this small park which survives behind its hedges, although the hipped-roofed shelter (left) has been removed. To the right and just out of view is the King George Field with its armorial gate piers dated 1936, now the site of Burton Latimer Community Centre as well as the playing fields.

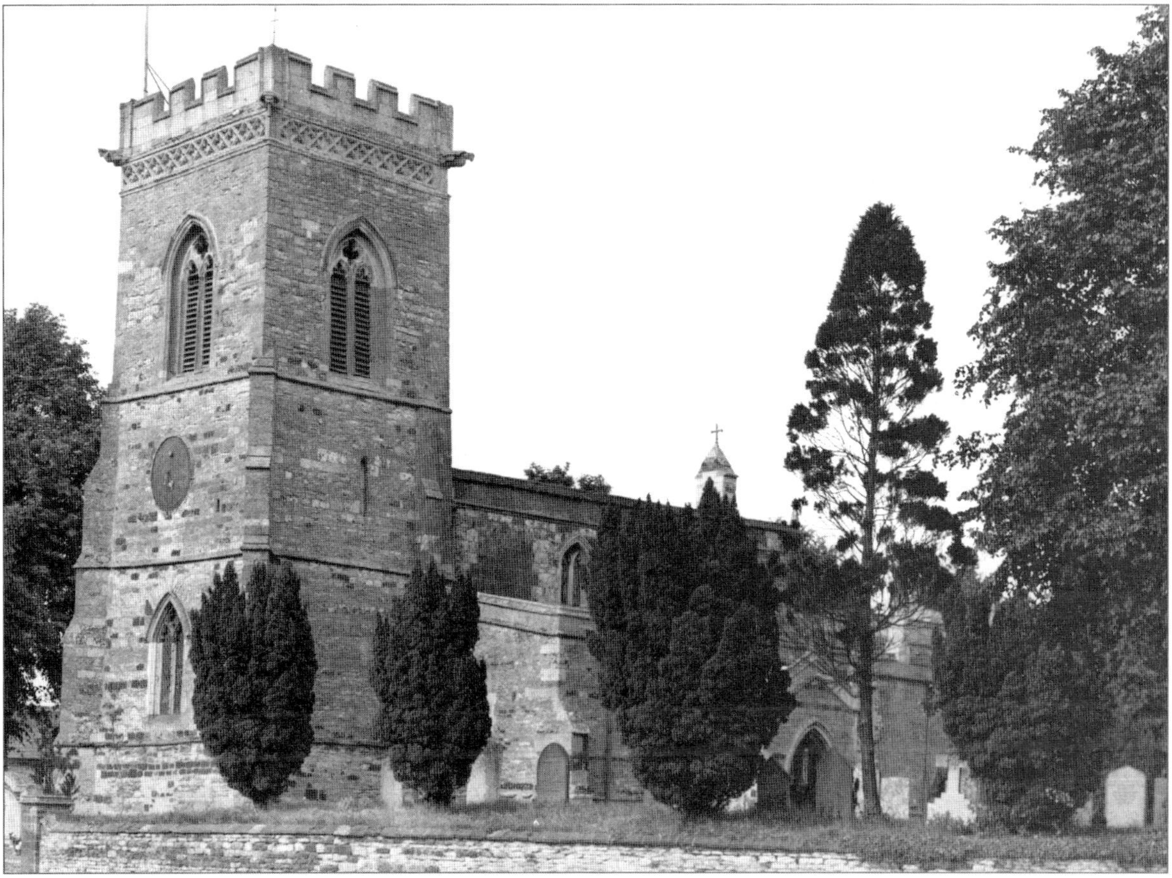

ISHAM, *The Parish Church c1955* I31036

The last visit on this first tour is to Isham, situated to the west of Burton Latimer and on the Wellingborough Road three miles south of Kettering. The best part of the village lies east of the Wellingborough Road, with the church close to the turning into South Street (view I31037 page 76). The church of St Peter contains some late Norman arcades, but for once the tower (of about 1350) does not have a spire. The tall trees to the right have now been felled, while the war memorial is the arched plaque to the left.

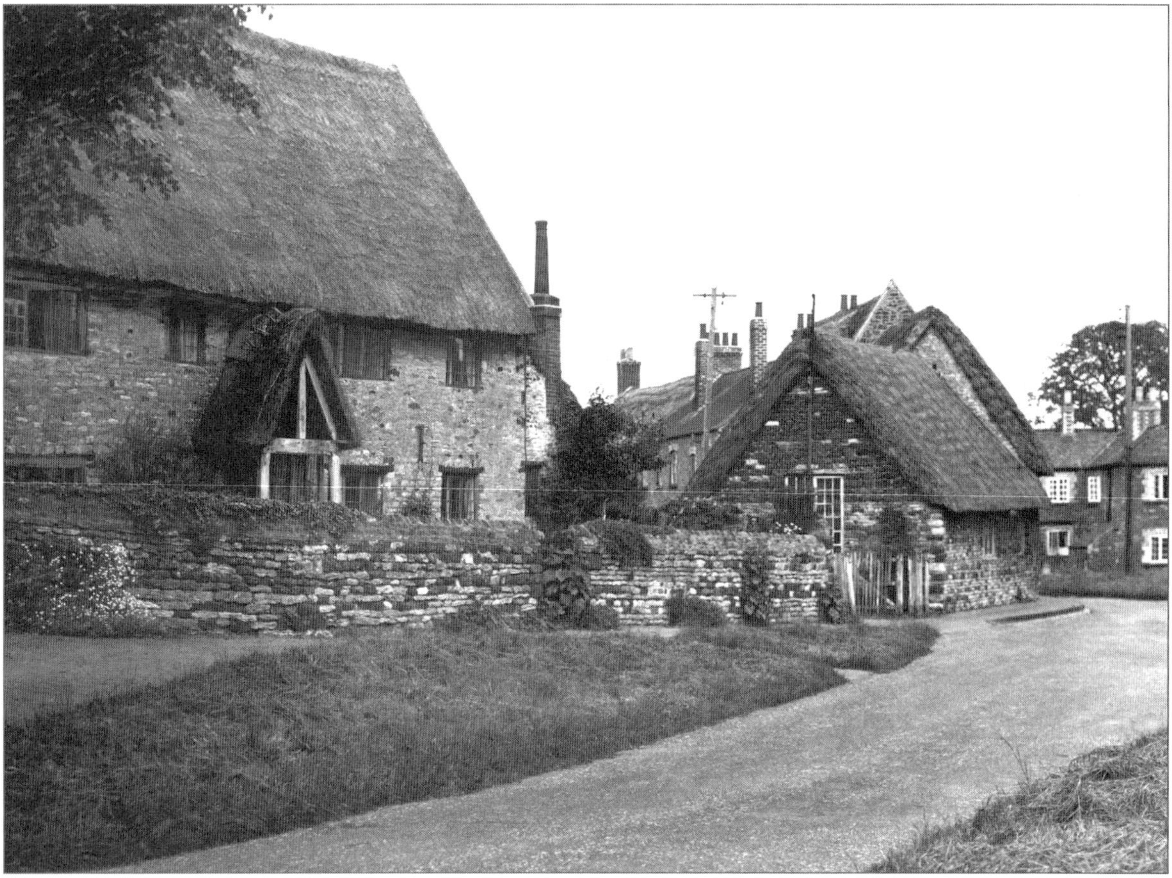

ISHAM

South Street c1955 I31037

Round the corner in South Street is Little Thatches (left), 18th-century rubblestone with its windows now painted white. The thatched building beyond has had its roof entirely removed and replaced by a flat one, and is converted to offices and named The Old Workshop. Opposite and just out of view on the right is a former stone tithe barn with a large arched central archway, now blocked, which has been converted into a house.

THE NENE VALLEY WEST OF WELLINGBOROUGH

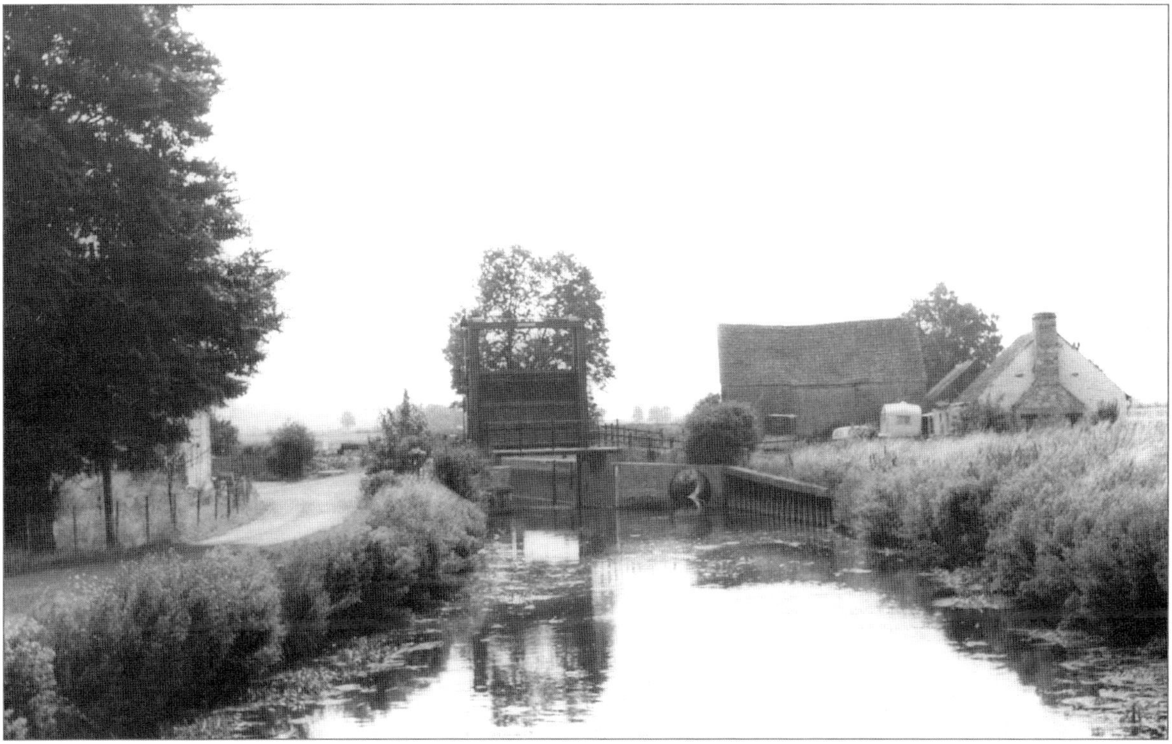

GREAT DODDINGTON
The River Nene c1960 G137010

The second tour from Wellingborough moves south-west down the Nene valley to Great Doddington. The village itself stands on higher ground some 125 feet above the valley floor. The first view, though, is on the river, taken from the bridge over it on the Hardwater Road. Behind the tree on the left, now felled, is Hardwater Mill, an 18th-century whitewashed building. This stretch of the Nene to Northampton from Thrapston was improved or 'navigated' in the 1750s and here by-passed the mill, although the huge raised sluice is later.

GREAT DODDINGTON
The High Street c1960
G137005

The village core is relatively small, but to the east housing along the north side of The Ridge almost links it to Wellingborough's outskirts, while estates have been developed to its west along the Earls Barton Road since World War II. This view looks west along the High Street towards the Church Lane turning. The stone and thatch 17th-century No 36 stands on the right, and beyond are various (then new) 1950s bungalows and houses. Beyond are the stone stacks of The Old Vicarage, a 17th-century house, formerly the manor house.

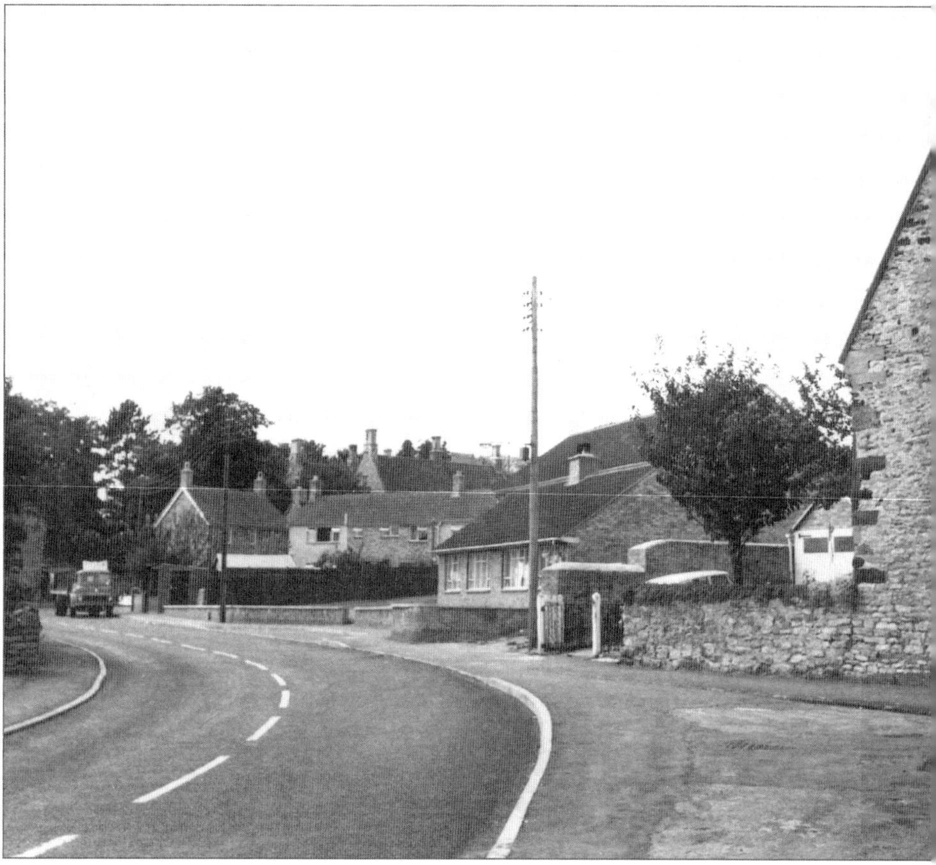

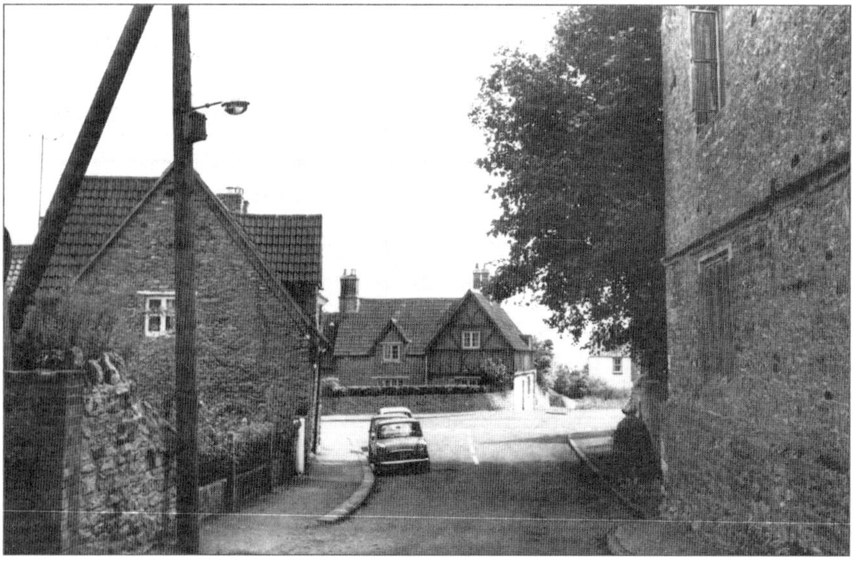

GREAT DODDINGTON
The Village c1960
G137003

Now a little further west, Frith's photographer was looking down Church Lane to the High Street. On the right is The Old Vicarage with its 17th-century stone mullioned windows; it used to be the manor house, and is now subdivided into three dwellings. Closing the view on the corner of Doctors Lane is another 17th-century stone cottage, this time with picturesque 19th-century timber framing applied to its right gabled wing.

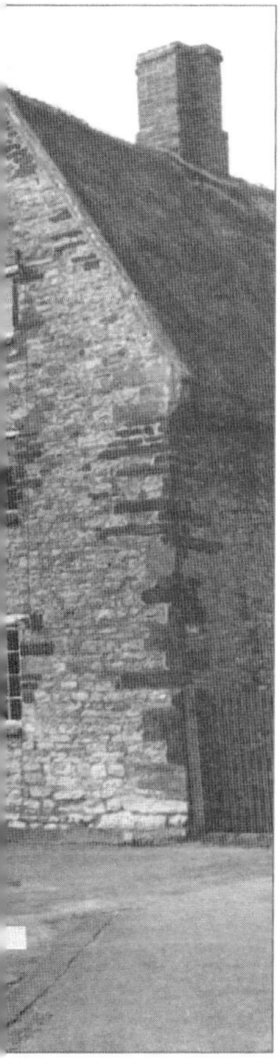

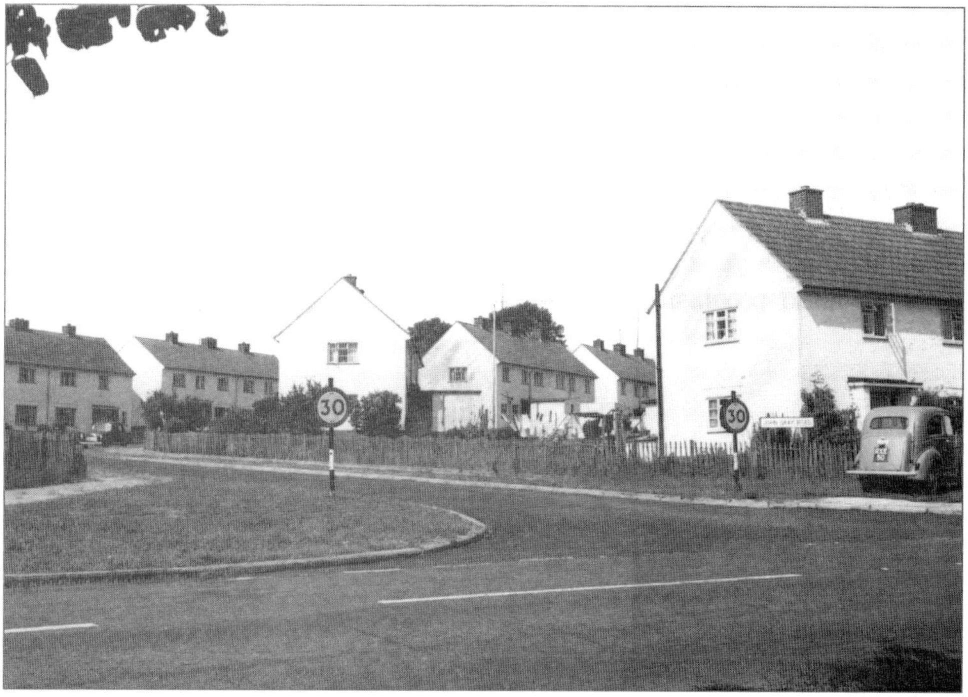

▲ **GREAT DODDINGTON,** *John Gray Road c1960* G137015

Further along the Earls Barton Road is this 1950s estate of council housing: it is simple and clean-lined, with painted brick walls and pantiled roofs, only a few years old at the time of the photograph. Since then virtually all the windows have been replaced by UPVC ones.

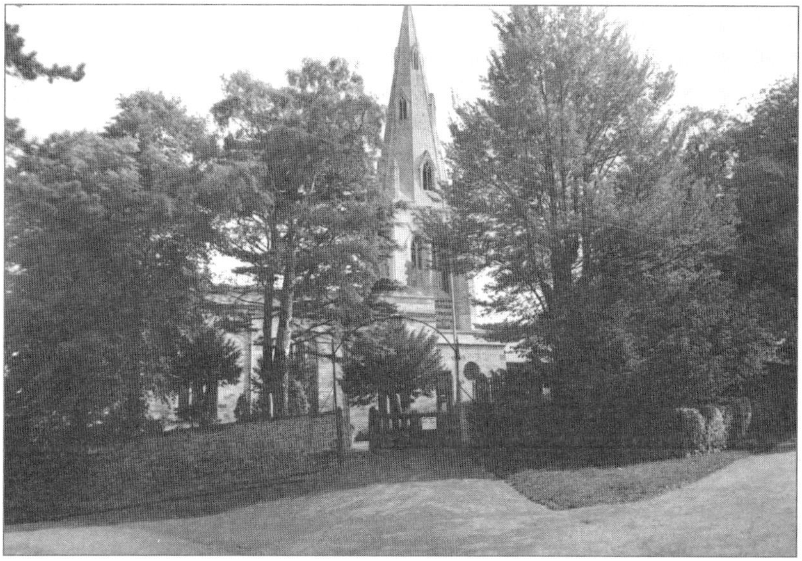

◄ **WOLLASTON**
The Parish Church c1955
W421012

Crossing the River Nene we head south-east to Wollaston, a small market town. Its market charter was granted in 1260, and it has the remains of a motte and bailey castle. Noted for lace making until the early 19th century, this industry was replaced by the ubiquitous boot and shoe industry of the area, and the stone village was surrounded by brick Victorian terraces built for the shoe workers, interspersed with shoe factories. The parish church at the top of Hickmire has a good medieval central tower and spire. The nave was rebuilt in 1737.

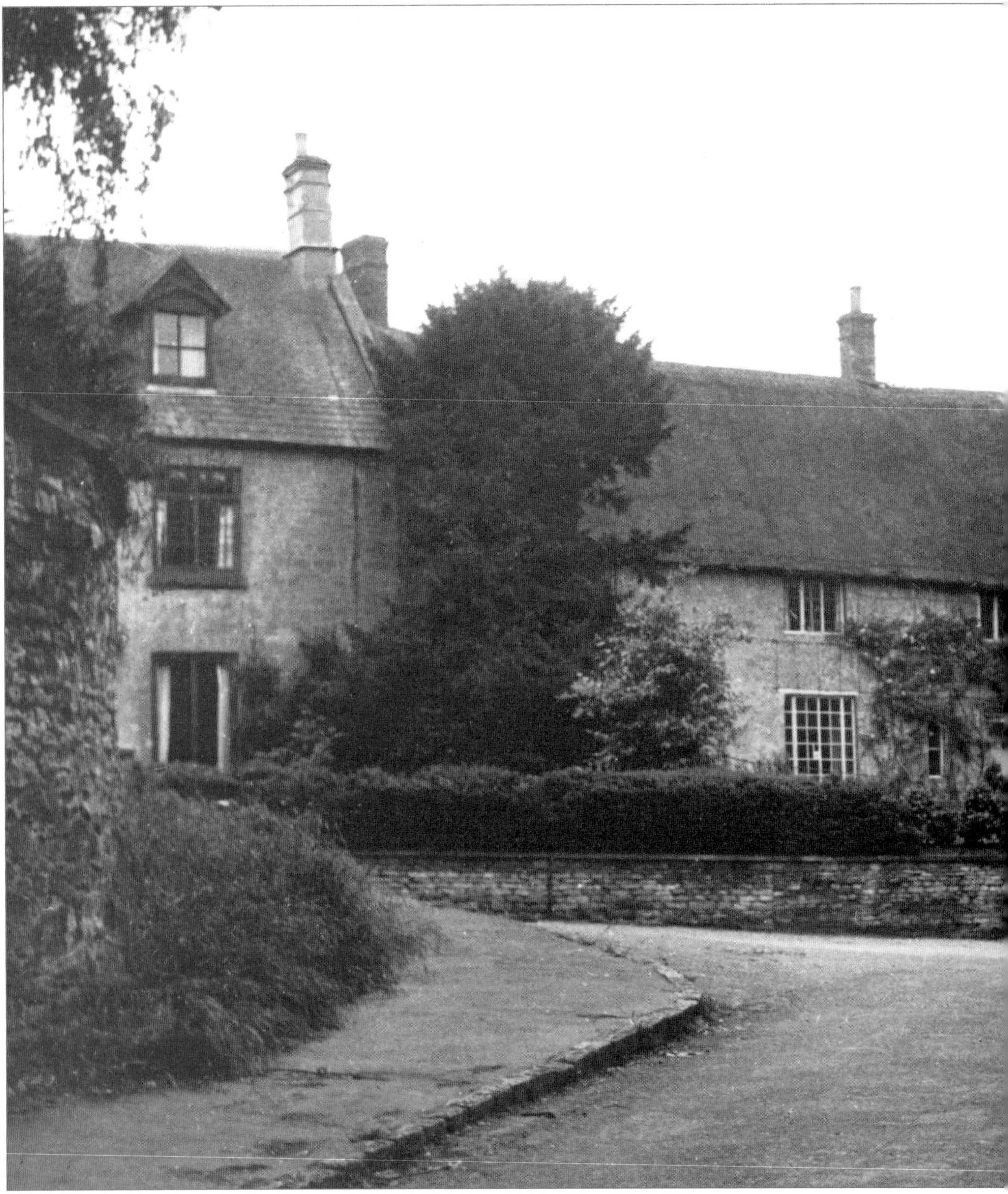

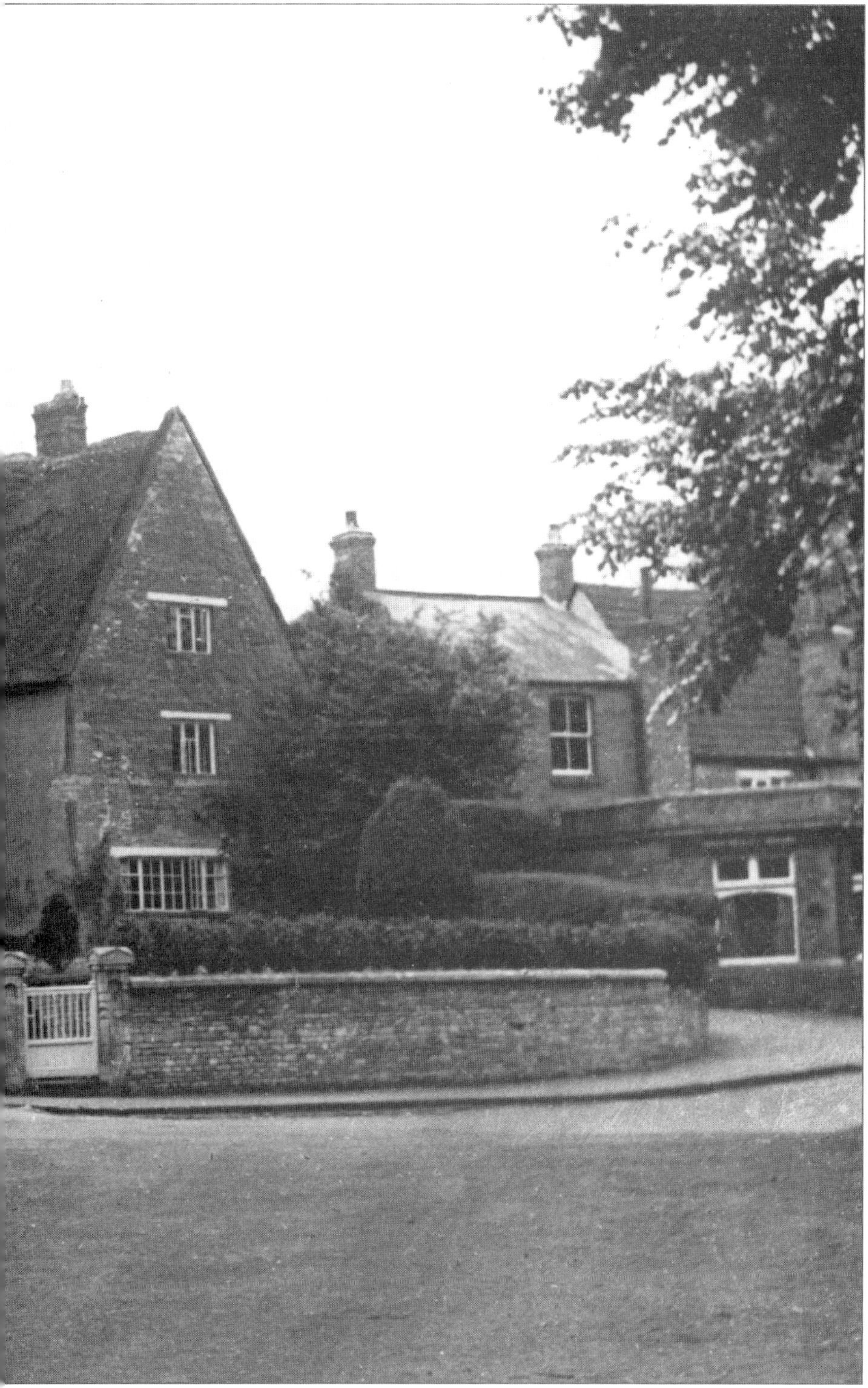

WOLLASTON
The Village c1955
W421002

This view looks along Hickmire, with the churchyard wall at the left. The central thatched building, dated 1680, is no longer a house - it is now The Hill Social Club; the 19th-century Cricketers pub stands to its right. The left turn leads to Wollaston Hall, built in 1738 and now the offices of Scott Bader, the polymer and plastics firm that came to Wollaston during World War II. The other major employers are Griggs, boot and shoe makers at Wollaston since 1911, who started producing Dr Martens cushion-sole shoes under licence from Germany in 1960.

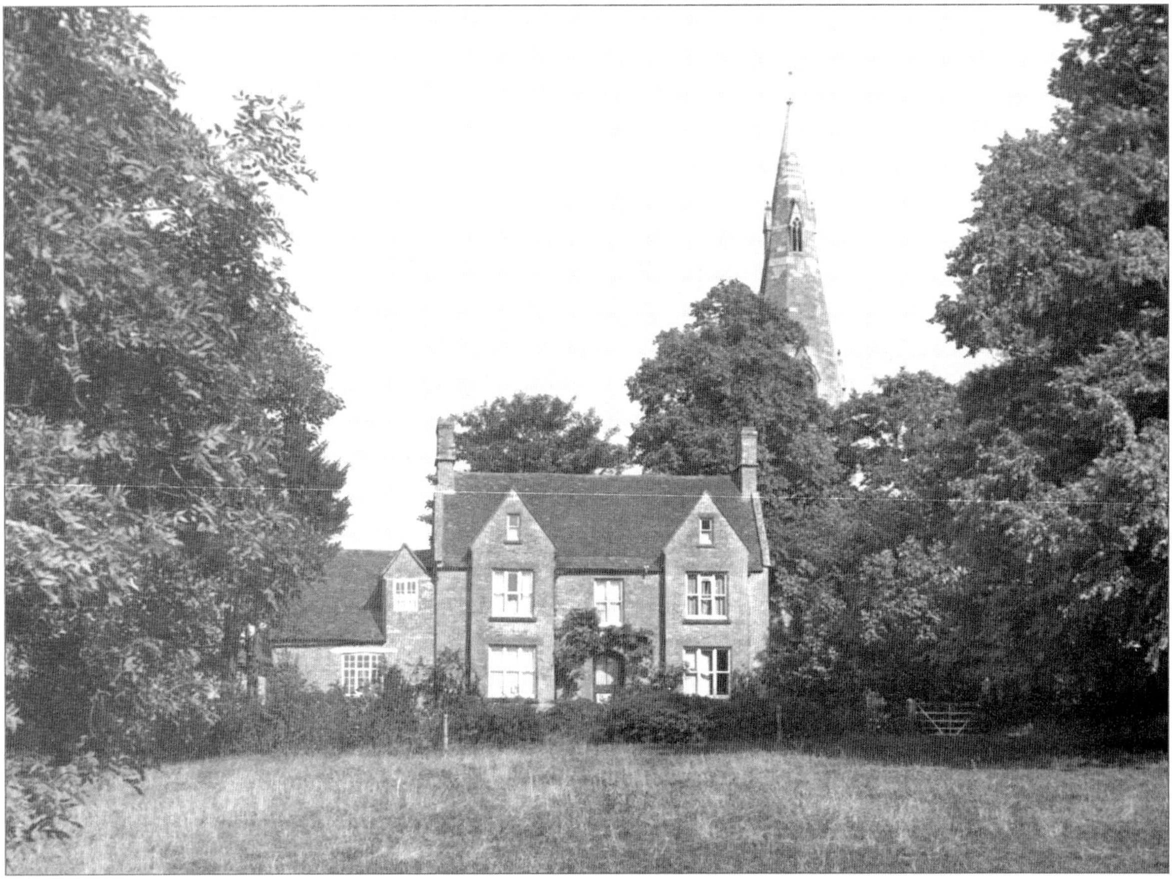

BOZEAT
The Vicarage c1960 B701004

A couple of miles south of Wollaston we reach Bozeat, now bypassed by the A609 from Wellingborough to Milton Keynes, and the last village in Northamptonshire before the road crosses the Buckinghamshire border. This view is from the paddock to the left of Hensman's Lane looking towards the spire of the parish church past the Victorian vicarage. The vicarage was demolished soon afterwards and replaced by a smaller buff brick one.

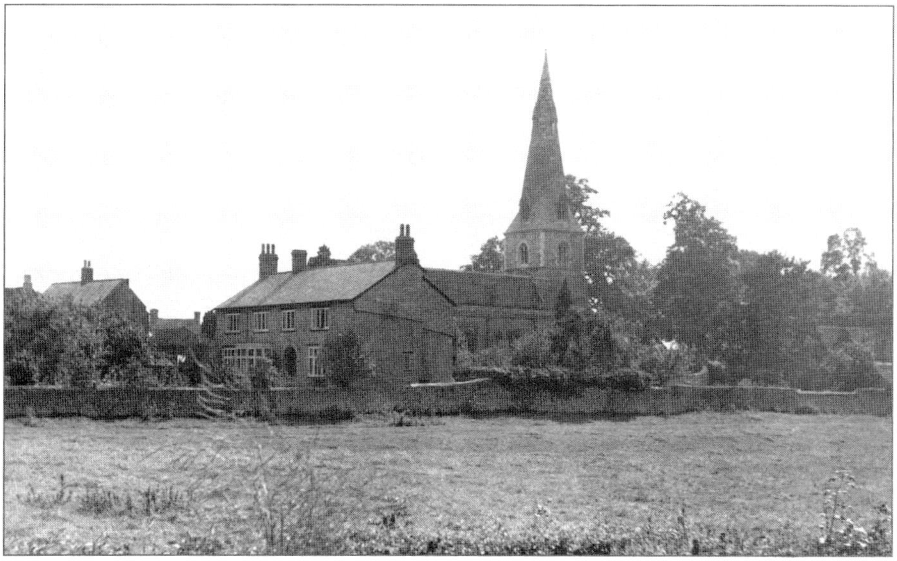

BOZEAT
The Parish Church c1955 B701007

Frith's photographer looks south-west from Allens Hill towards the church across a nowadays somewhat curtailed paddock. In front of the church is Stoneleigh, a late 19th-century stone-built house with a long stone boundary wall fronting the paddock. St Mary's Church has a late Norman tower and a 14th-century spire, both rebuilt in the 1880s.

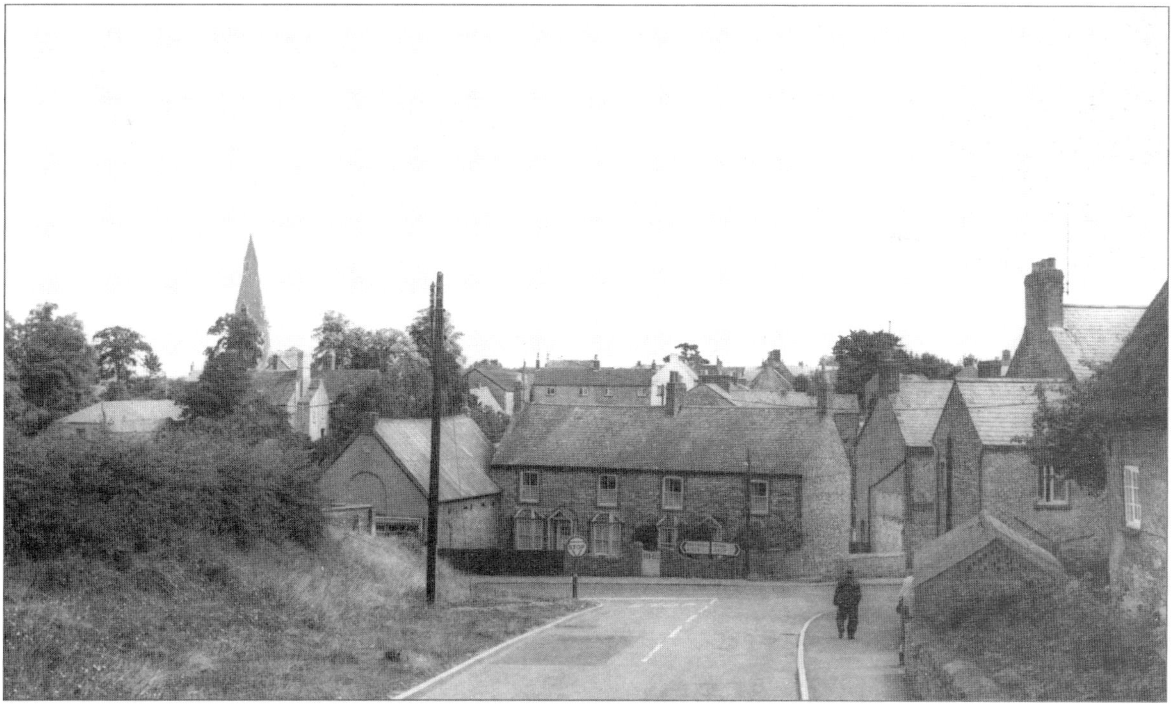

BOZEAT, *Easton Lane c1960* B701017

Now west of the church, Frith's photographer looks down Easton Lane towards London Road. Easton Lane is now blocked by a grass area and bollards, and a new stretch of road joins London Road further to the left. This avoids the dangerous junction. Indeed, road improvement after 1960 demolished a number of cottages at the High Street junction, including the one with the raking drainpipe beyond the walking man (right).

BOZEAT
Camden Square c1960
B701020

Camden Square is at the east end of Bozeat's High Street at the crossroads, continuing straight on into Dychurch Lane. At the left is the village school, built in 1872; since this view was taken, it has been converted into a house behind high hedges. The shop on the right is now Bozeat Post Office.

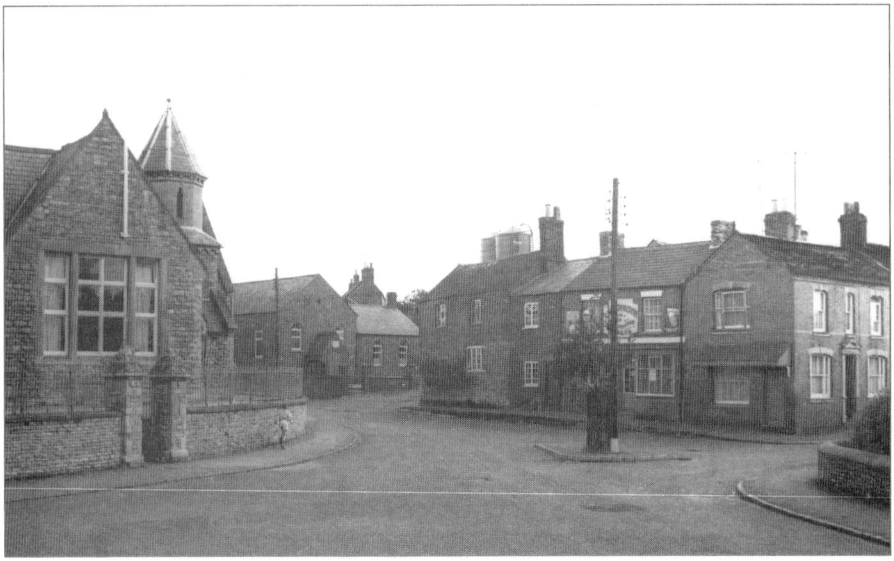

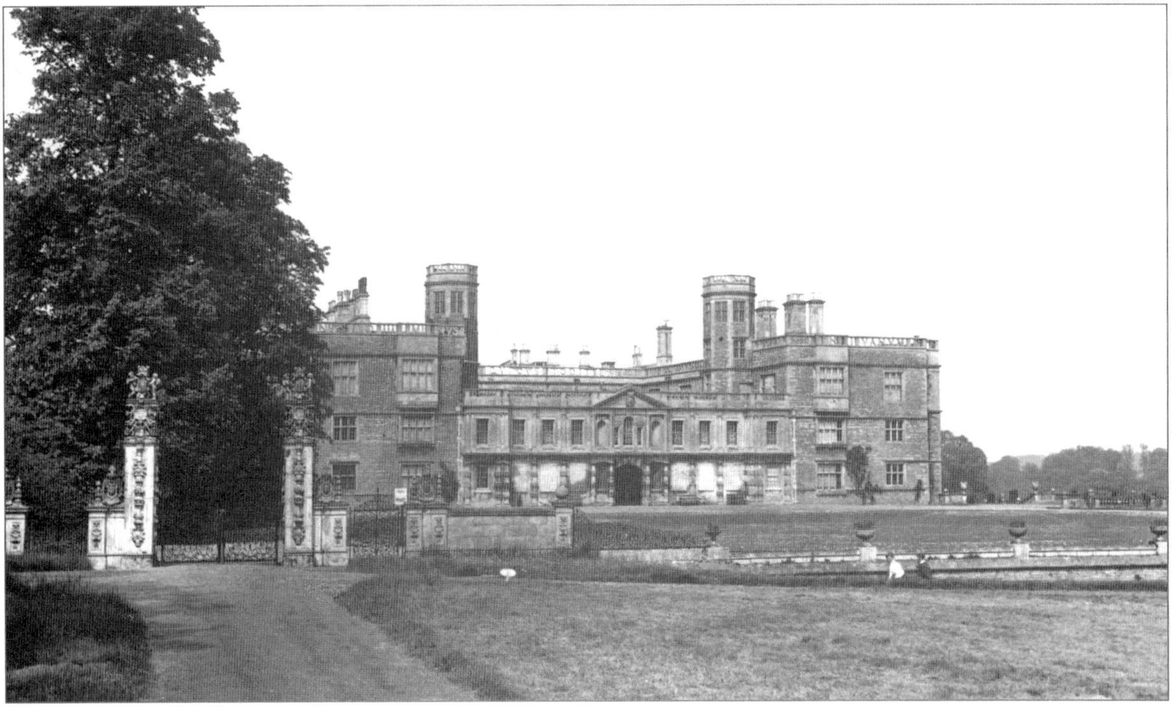

CASTLE ASHBY, *The House c1955* C224002

Two miles west of Bozeat, and definitely out of boot and shoe country, we reach one of Northamptonshire's largest landed estates. At its heart stands a vast Elizabethan mansion which replaced the eponymous castle. It was started in 1574 by the Comptons, who later became Earls of Northampton. Completed in the early 17th century, it is famous for its unusual 1624 balustrade: in place of balusters, it has letters forming a quotation from Psalm 127.

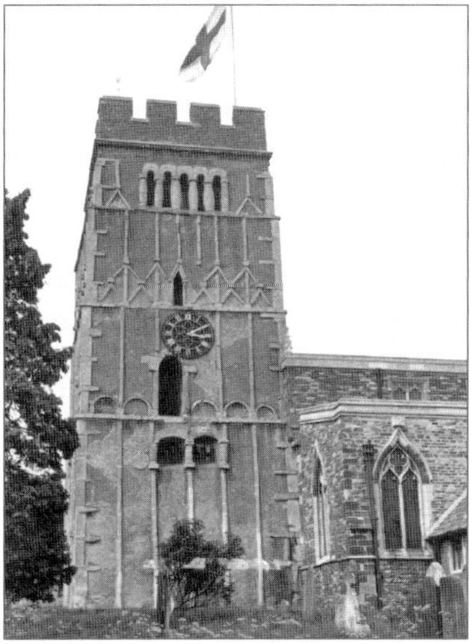

EARLS BARTON
The Parish Church c1955 E97006

From the vast acres of the landscaped park of Castle Ashby this brief tour re-crosses the river Nene to the north side to visit Earls Barton, the last visit to a boot and shoe town in this book. At the heart of the town is the Anglo-Saxon parish church; the bulk of the rest of the town is Victorian and 20th century. The church, with its west tower of about AD970, is one of a fine group of Northamptonshire churches that were built after the Anglo-Saxon re-conquest of the Danelaw in the first half of the 10th century.

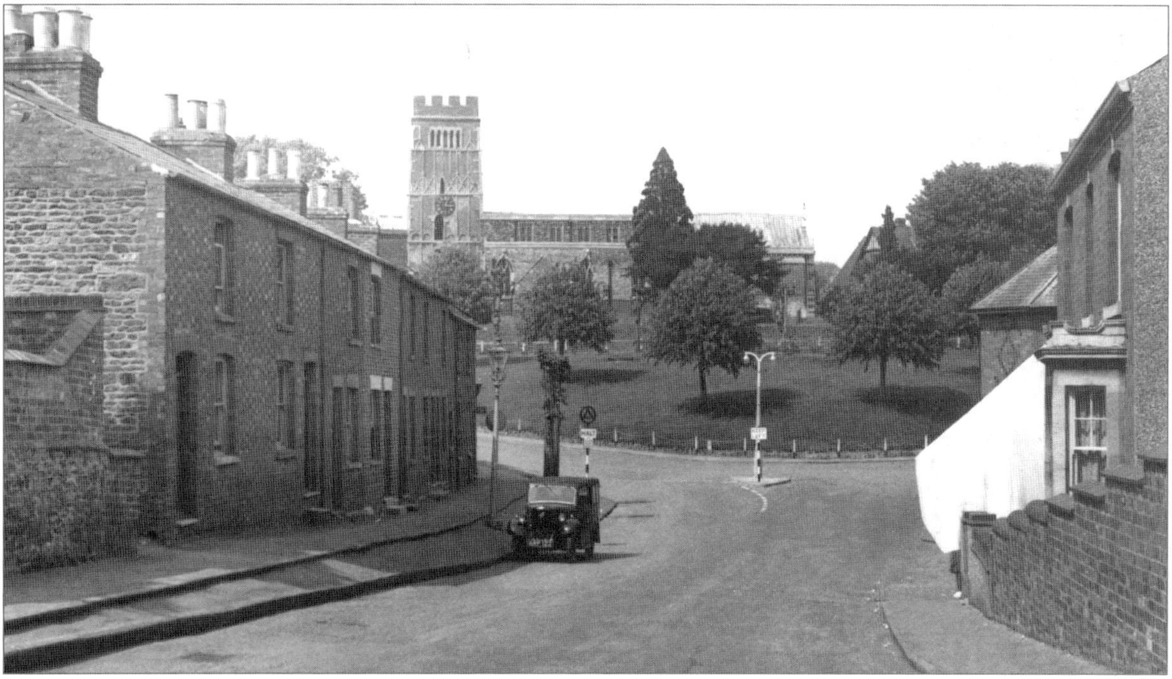

EARLS BARTON, *Station Road c1955* E97008

The church occupies the end of a low ridge, and behind it are the mound and earthworks of a good example of a Norman motte and bailey castle. In this view the dominance of the Anglo-Saxon west tower of the church can be clearly seen. Station Road is no longer a strictly accurate name, for the station, which opened in 1845 nearer the river, was closed in the 1960s. The tracks of the line from Blisworth to join the Midland Railway at Wellingborough were lifted after the line closed to freight in 1972.

EARLS BARTON
The Square c1955 E97009

Frith's photographer is looking south in the opposite direction to view E97008 (page 85) from the grassed slope below the church towards Station Road - The Corner Shop stands on the left. The car is turning left into Harcourt Square, where a former shoe factory has been converted into flats and workshops, Harcourt Mews. The shop with the blind is now a Londis store, and the stepped garden wall beyond belongs to almshouses built in 1832 and 'reconstructed' in 1961. Note the elegant 1950s concrete street lamps, now long gone.

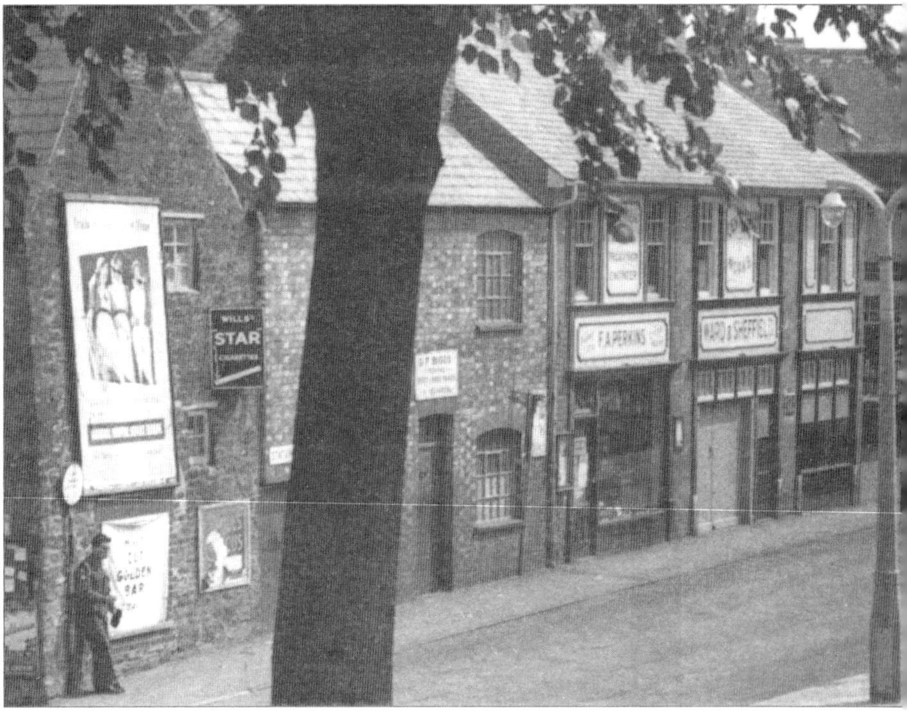

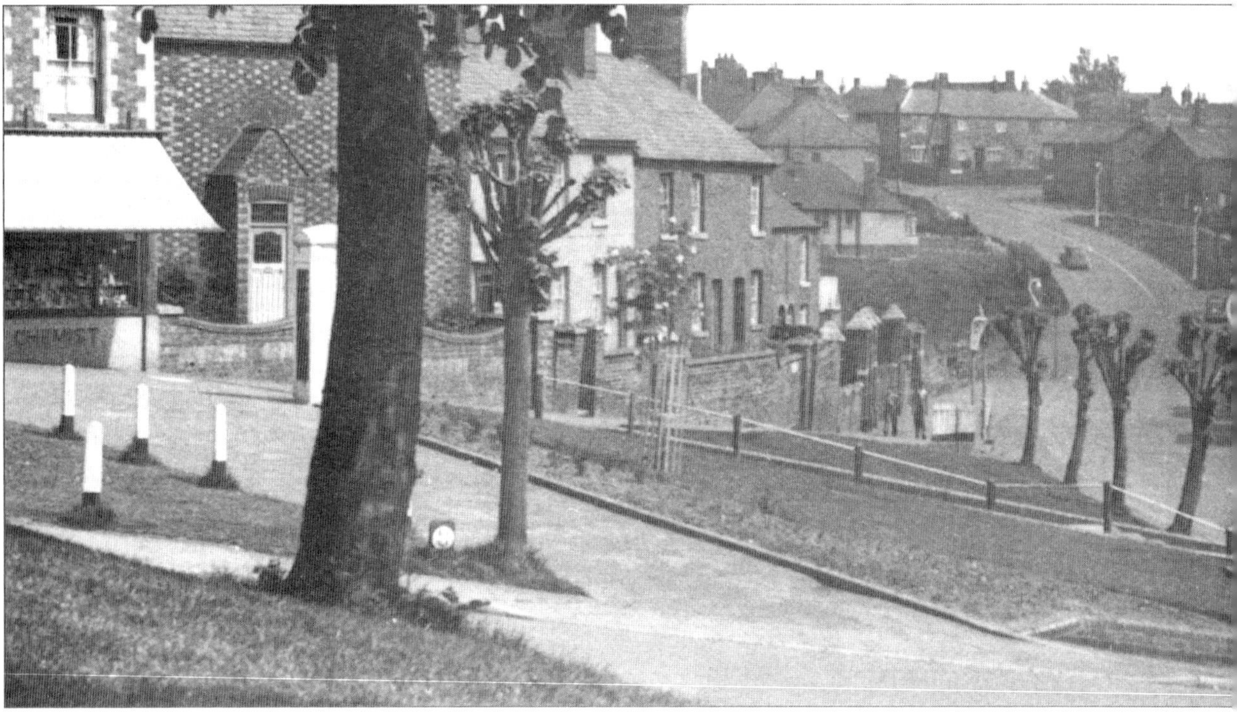

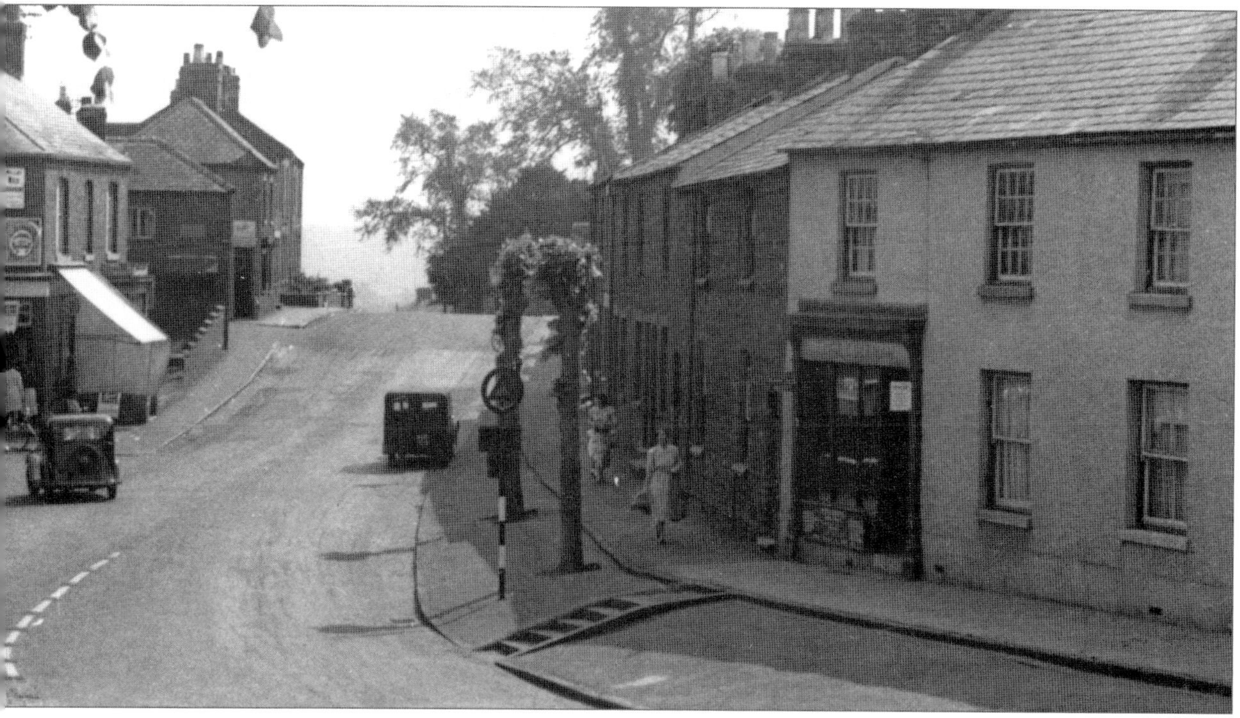

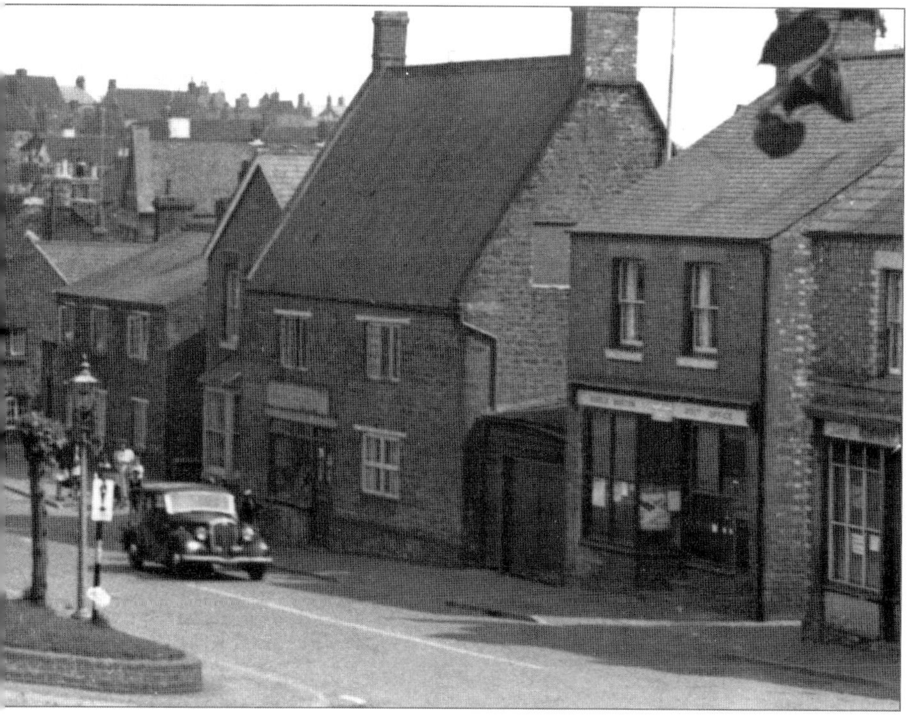

◄ **EARLS BARTON**
Broad Street c1955 E97010

Turning east, Frith's photographer is looking from The Square into Broad Street. The High Street climbs to the left in the foreground towards the castle earthworks and a supermarket. The shop with the blind (left) is still a chemist's, David Jeyes, and a Museum of Village Life.
To the right is the post office with an 18th-century thatched and stone-built house, Vine Cottage, as a reminder of the pre-boot and shoe village when it was known for lace-making, tanning and rush matting.

MOULTON

Church Street c1955 M295006

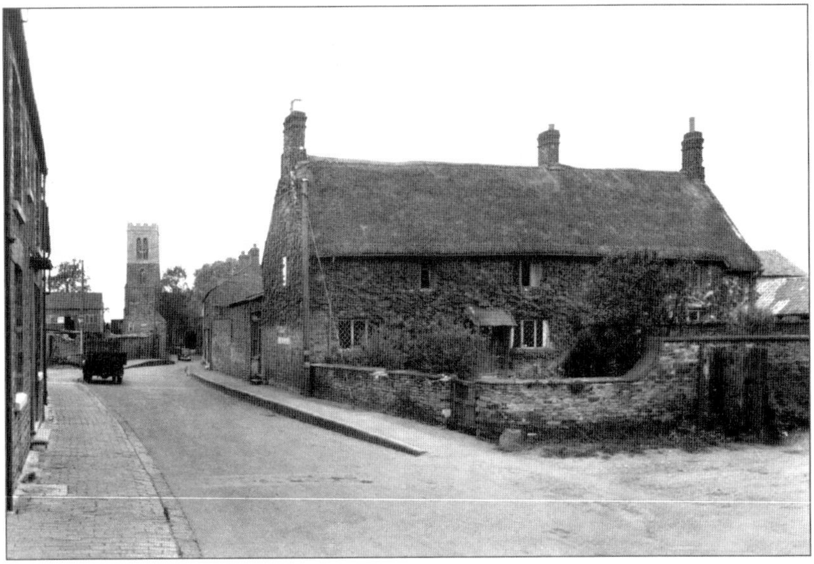

The last village visited in this chapter is situated north-west of Earls Barton and is now reached via the northward expansion of Northampton itself. It is a village of winding lanes of such a narrowness that now many of them are one-way and baffling to car-borne visitors. Church Street is one of those one-way streets. The tall parish church tower, 14th-century with a 15th-century belfry stage, rises in the distance. The farm access lane on the right is now the access road to a 1960s housing estate, Parade Bank, and the thatched 18th-century farmhouse has been restored.

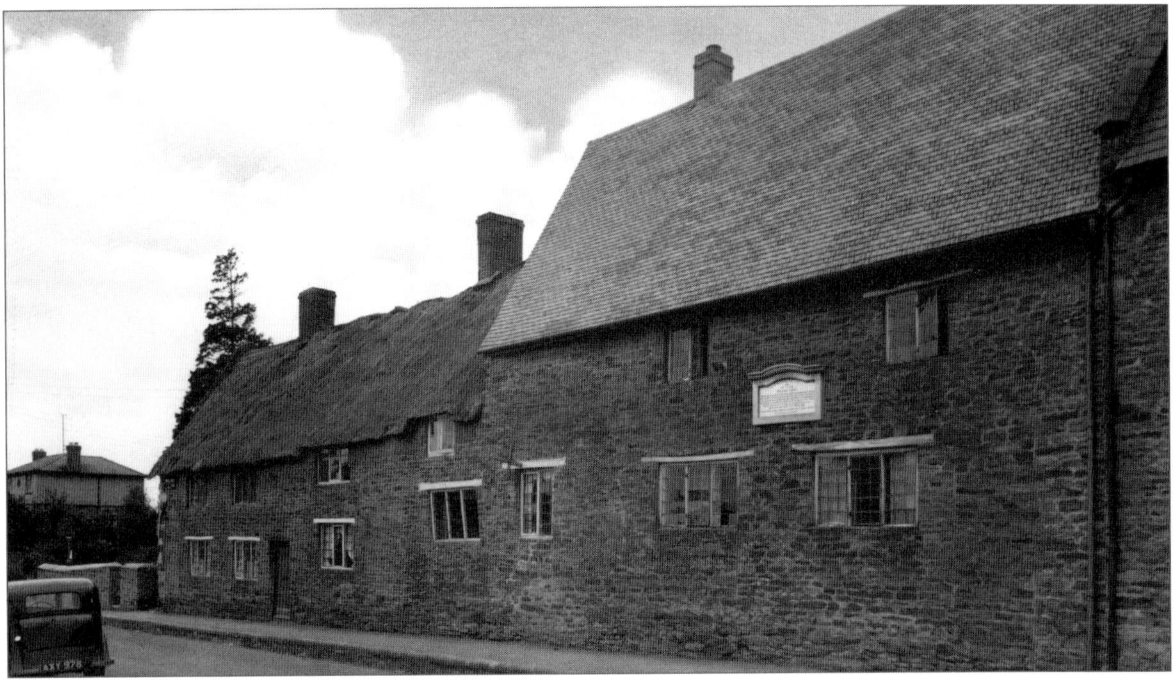

MOULTON, *William Carey's Cottage, West Street c1955* M295005

Here in West Street we see the cottage (with the plaque) where the Reverend William Carey lived from 1785-89. He was a founder of the Baptist Missionary Society. Born in Paulerspury in 1761, Carey was originally a shoemaker, then a minister and scholar. Indeed, he translated the Bible into many Indian languages and died in India in 1834. The cottages to the left, in a poor state in the 1950s, have since been demolished, revealing more of the Carey Baptist Church behind them which had been enlarged in 1879.

INDEX

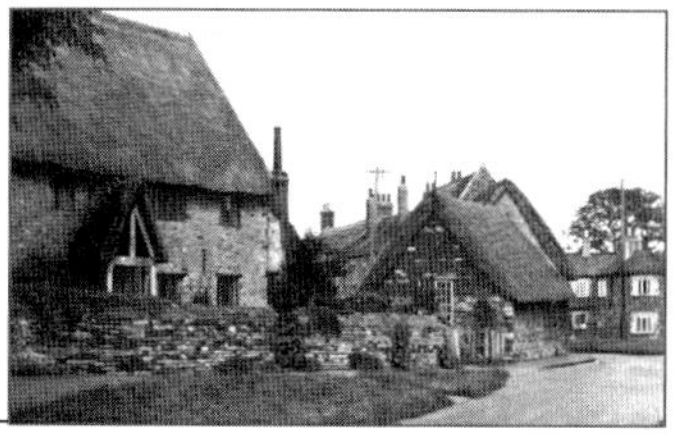

NAMES OF SUBSCRIBERS

The following people have kindly supported this book by subscribing to copies before publication.

Mr Robin Adams, Wellingborough

Mr S. Bean

Mr D. Bonsall

Jennifer Brundage

Kerri, Carol & Corey Burgess

Adam Chambers 3rd July 2004

The Chapman Family

Donald Claridge, Wellingborough

Mr Eric Peter Coles, Wellingborough

Jillian Cook, Princess Way

The Darnell Family, Wellingborough

Mr & Mrs Diserens

Mr & Mrs M. J. Dolan, Wellingborough

M. & G. Doyle

Teresa & Robert du Feu, Wellingborough

Brian C. Dunkley, Wellingborough

In Memory of T. E. Farden

Pamela Field, Great Doddington

Mr Dennis Furnell & Mrs Eleanor Furnell

Mrs R. Gleed-Owen

J. C. Holloway, Wellingborough

Mr John & Mrs Jean Houghton, Wellingborough

Jill Kaczmaryk and Family

The Kaczmaryk Family, Vivian Road, Wellingborough

Mr & Mrs Kendal

T. & M. McDermont

Andrew McGonigle

George McGuire

Peggy Miller

Mrs Ella Mitchell

The Murphy Family, Wellingborough

Henry Newcombe, Wollaston

The O'Brien Family, Wellingborough

Cherie O'Hagan, Wellingborough

In Memory of Beatrice Owen

Mrs I. D. Pepin

John W. Shaw, Wellingborough

Mr S. M. & Mrs T. A. Smith, Wellingborough

The Sorrell Family, USA

Mary & Ray Stapleton

Raymond & Lisa Stewart

Sam Stuart

The Tate Family, Wellingborough

Mr D. M. & Mrs L. J. Thomas, Wellingborough

Lynne & Roger Underwood, Irchester

George A. Vickers 2004

Pat Ward, Irthlinboro

David Westley, Wellingborough

Mark G. Winters, Wellingborough

Helen Wright

Frith Products & Services

Francis Frith would doubtless be pleased to know that the pioneering publishing venture he started in 1860 still continues today. Over a hundred and forty years later, The Francis Frith Collection continues in the same innovative tradition and is now one of the foremost publishers of vintage photographs in the world. Some of the current activities include:

Interior Decoration

Today Frith's photographs can be seen framed and as giant wall murals in thousands of pubs, restaurants, hotels, banks, retail stores and other public buildings throughout the country. In every case they enhance the unique local atmosphere of the places they depict and provide reminders of gentler days in an increasingly busy and frenetic world.

Product Promotions

Frith products are used by many major companies to promote the sales of their own products or to reinforce their own history and heritage. Frith promotions have been used by Hovis bread, Courage beers, Scots Porage Oats, Colman's mustard, Cadbury's foods, Mellow Birds coffee, Dunhill pipe tobacco, Guinness, and Bulmer's Cider.

Genealogy and Family History

As the interest in family history and roots grows world-wide, more and more people are turning to Frith's photographs of Great Britain for images of the towns, villages and streets where their ancestors lived; and, of course, photographs of the churches and chapels where their ancestors were christened, married and buried are an essential part of every genealogy tree and family album.

Frith Products

All Frith photographs are available Framed or just as Mounted Prints and Posters (size 23 x 16 inches). These may be ordered from the address below. From time to time other products - Address Books, Calendars, Table Mats, etc - are available.

The Internet

Already fifty thousand Frith photographs can be viewed and purchased on the internet through the Frith websites and a myriad of partner sites.

For more detailed information on Frith companies and products, look at these sites:

www.francisfrith.co.uk
www.francisfrith.com
(for North American visitors)

See the complete list of Frith Books at:

www.francisfrith.co.uk

This web site is regularly updated with the latest list of publications from the Frith Book Company. If you wish to buy books relating to another part of the country that your local bookshop does not stock, you may purchase on-line.

For further information, trade, or author enquiries please contact us at the address below:

The Francis Frith Collection, Frith's Barn, Teffont, Salisbury, Wiltshire, England SP3 5QP.
Tel: +44 (0)1722 716 376 Fax: +44 (0)1722 716 881 Email: sales@francisfrith.co.uk

See Frith books on the internet at www.francisfrith.co.uk

FREE MOUNTED PRINT

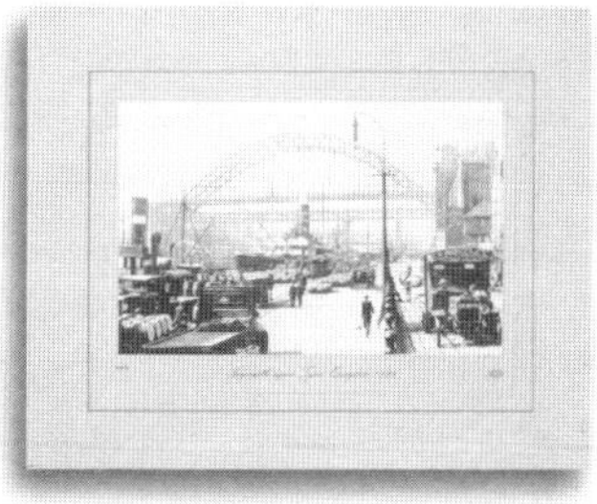

Mounted Print
Overall size 14 x 11 inches

Fill in and cut out this voucher and return *it with your remittance for £2.25 (to cover postage and handling). Offer valid for delivery to UK addresses only.*

Choose any photograph included in this book. *Your SEPIA print will be A4 in size. It will be mounted in a cream mount with a burgundy rule line (overall size 14 x 11 inches).*

Order additional Mounted Prints at HALF PRICE (only £7.49 each*)
If you would like to order more Frith prints from this book, possibly as gifts for friends and family, you can buy them at half price (with no additional postage and handling costs).

Have your Mounted Prints framed
For an extra £14.95 per print* you can have your mounted print(s) framed in an elegant polished wood and gilt moulding, overall size 16 x 13 inches (no additional postage and handling required).

*** IMPORTANT!**

These special prices are only available if you order at the same time as you order your free mounted print. You must use the ORIGINAL VOUCHER on this page (no copies permitted). We can only despatch to one address.

Send completed Voucher form to:
The Francis Frith Collection, Frith's Barn, Teffont, Salisbury, Wiltshire SP3 5QP

CHOOSE ANY IMAGE FROM THIS BOOK

Voucher
*for **FREE** and Reduced Price Frith Prints*

Please do not photocopy this voucher. Only the original is valid, so please fill it in, cut it out and return it to us with your order.

Picture ref no	Page no	Qty	Mounted @ £7.49	Framed + £14.95	Total Cost
		1	Free of charge*	£	£
			£7.49	£	£
			£7.49	£	£
			£7.49	£	£
			£7.49	£	£
			£7.49	£	£
Please allow 28 days for delivery			* Post & handling (UK)		£2.25
			Total Order Cost		£

Title of this book . . . .
I enclose a cheque/postal order for £ . . . .
made payable to 'The Francis Frith Collection'

OR please debit my Mastercard / Visa / Switch / Amex card
(credit cards please on all overseas orders), details below

Card Number

Issue No (Switch only) Valid from (Amex/Switch)

Expires Signature

Name Mr/Mrs/Ms ....
Address ....
....
....
.... Postcode ....
Daytime Tel No ....
Email ....

Valid to 31/12/05

Free Print - see overleaf

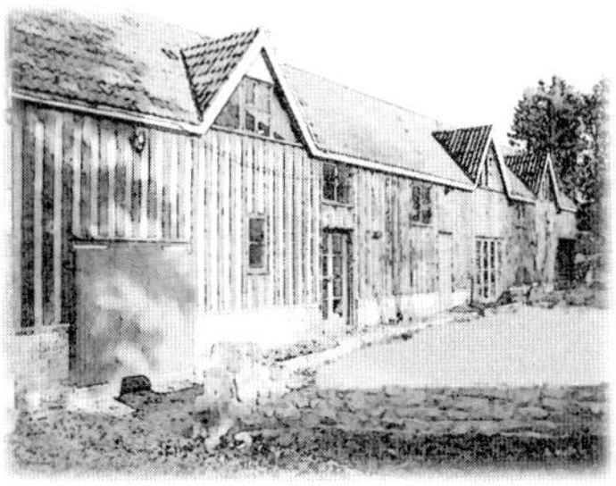

Would you like to find out more about Francis Frith?

We have recently recruited some entertaining speakers who are happy to visit local groups, clubs and societies to give an illustrated talk documenting Frith's travels and photographs. If you are a member of such a group and are interested in hosting a presentation, we would love to hear from you.

Our speakers bring with them a small selection of our local town and county books, together with sample prints. They are happy to take orders. A small proportion of the order value is donated to the group who have hosted the presentation. The talks are therefore an excellent way of fundraising for small groups and societies.

Can you help us with information about any of the Frith photographs in this book?

We are gradually compiling an historical record for each of the photographs in the Frith archive. It is always fascinating to find out the names of the people shown in the pictures, as well as insights into the shops, buildings and other features depicted.

If you recognize anyone in the photographs in this book, or if you have information not already included in the author's caption, do let us know. We would love to hear from you, and will try to publish it in future books or articles.

Our production team

Frith books are produced by a small dedicated team at offices in the converted Grade II listed 18th-century barn at Teffont near Salisbury, illustrated above. Most have worked with the Frith Collection for many years. All have in common one quality: they have a passion for the Frith Collection. The team is constantly expanding, but currently includes:

Jason Buck, John Buck, Ruth Butler, Heather Crisp, David Davies, Isobel Hall, Julian Hight, Peter Horne, James Kinnear, Karen Kinnear, Tina Leary, Stuart Login, Amanda Lowe, David Marsh, Sue Molloy, Kate Rotondetto, Dean Scource, Eliza Sackett, Terence Sackett, Sandra Sampson, Adrian Sanders, Sandra Sanger, Julia Skinner, Claire Tarrier, Lewis Taylor, Shelley Tolcher and Lorraine Tuck.